The Walshes came full circle, bringing their journey with dogs back to the exact place where it started—on Atwood Street in Wellesley, Massachusetts. Bob Walsh is sitting on the same spot on the stoop where he was photographed seventy years before. As you can see, the little boy who was pictured with his mother, twin brother, sister, and first dog back in 1941, returned as a mature man with his own family in 2011. It's only fitting they brought their current dogs to re-create the picture, including Beverly the German Shepherd, who played a major role in leading the Walsh family home.

Albert

Dee Dee
Smooth Fox Terrier Mix

Marie Beth

Frisky
Mongrel

Poker
Cocker Spaniel

Bob

Fly Boy & Claudia
Cocker Spaniel

Richard

Albert & Elizabeth
WALSH

Bob & Carole
WALSH

Christopher

Murphy
St. Bernard

Daisy #1
Cairn Terrier

Kevin

Danielle
Cairn Terrier

Susie Marie
Golden Retriever

Daisy #2
Dalmatian

Annie
Pembroke Welsh Corgi

Michael

Chris & Suzanne
WALSH

Raley
Shih Tzu

Daisy #3
Yellow Lab

Rio
Black Lab

Samantha

Tiffany
German Shepherd

Beverly
German Shepherd

Amanda

Kevin & Jean
WALSH

Tyler

Caitlyn

Christopher

Anne

Peter

Georgia
Doberman Mix

Mike & Rachel
WALSH

FOLLOW *the* DOG HOME

FOLLOW
the DOG
HOME

How a simple walk

unleashed an incredible

family journey

BOB, SAMANTHA
and KEVIN WALSH

Boston, Massachusetts

ISBN13: 978-0-9839012-1-1
Library of Congress Control Number: 2011937295

Sweet Tea Books
PO Box 812748
Wellesley, MA 02482
www.FollowTheDogHome.com
www.Facebook.com/FollowTheDogHome

Printed in the United States
10 9 8 7 6 5 4 3 2 1

*For our fathers who had the wisdom to raise us with dogs,
and the dogs who blessed us with companionship, love,
and a lifetime of joy.*

Contents

Introduction

INTRODUCTION

Dogs are bridges to our past and our future, connecting people and generations like nothing else can, and nothing else will. They are institutions that have stood the test of time and transcend individual life. It doesn't get much better than experiencing a parent's joy in seeing his or her child fall in love with a puppy. A grandparent can brim with pride too, knowing he or she set that stage decades earlier with a similar canine gift. This is your father's world, to borrow the expression—or at least part of it can be, if you have a dog in your life.

It's our guess you love dogs as much as we do. Many of us were born with faithful pooches sharing our lives, memories, and family photos. Others developed a love along the way and embraced the concept of dogs as our best friends. We wondered about dogs as best friends and whether there was more to it. The answer is yes, absolutely yes, and we can prove it in a unique and loving way.

We're obviously not alone in our thoughts. Thirty-nine percent of American households own at least one dog, according to the Humane Society of the United States. Twenty-four percent own two dogs. So there are almost 78 million dogs living in American homes. Worldwide, the numbers vary, but 200 million pet dogs is a reasonable estimate. Clearly, dog owners have been—and always will be—on to something special. When a dog is with us, we're all on equal footing and get about the same thing out of it. We love the dog; the dog loves us. It's common ground.

Dogs ground us when time and technology change us in almost every facet of life. Their needs are so simple. We give them food, shelter, exercise, discipline, and love. They give us all the love back, plus devotion, loyalty, protection, and companionship. Nothing, absolutely nothing, has changed about this animal-human bond since humans started taking dogs into their homes thousands of years ago. How do you not like that?

Follow the Dog Home is the story of three generations of the Walsh family, and how dogs were a common thread that held us together when the events of our lives and the world threatened to pull us apart. Dogs were there for the most profoundly transformational moments of our lives: birth, death, job loss, and relocation. What's more they witnessed bathroom scenes, parties, and every embarrassing moment conceivable. We're just glad they can't talk. As you read, you'll probably substitute your own special memories of life with your dogs, and how they were far more than pets; they were family.

Writing a book with family members provides some interesting challenges. Different people have different opinions, styles of writing, and interpretations of what is said, how it's said, and what should be left unsaid. Part of it is personality, some of it is generational.

Authors Bob, Samantha, and Kevin Walsh

•   •   •

Kevin: *"Dad, really, whaddaya got against the word poop?"*

Bob "Grandpops": *"No, no, no. I just don't like it. It's not appropriate. If you have to talk about it, say 'droppings,' 'animal waste,' or 'excrement.' "*

Samantha: *"Oh that's so stuffy, Grandpops. I say poop so I don't say another bad word. We say it all the time in my house. Hah, hah, hah!"*

Amanda: *"Hey guys, when you're done talking about poop and your book project, can we dress Beverly up like a princess?"*

Bob "Grandpops" *(laughing): "What ... huh ... huh ... are you serious? She doesn't let you do that, does she?"*

Amanda: *"Of course she does. Beverly loves to play dress up."*

Bob "Grandpops": *"I'll believe it when I see it."*

Kevin: *"You'll see, Dad."*

Amanda, Beverly (Princess), and Samantha Walsh, 2010

So, as you can imagine, we had a few creative disagreements while writing our story. The good news is that we're still a family. Those creative disagreements led to careful thought, introspection, provocative discussion, and writing. That's how it ought to be. You'll see what we're talking about in the pages to come.

Kevin, Samantha, and Bob Walsh (dogs: Beverly and Annie)

Now, meet us. We have written *Follow the Dog Home* in three primary voices: There's seventy-two-year-old curmudgeonly Bob Walsh, who's often referred to as Grandpops or Dad (he's really a teddy bear, but don't tell him that). Kevin Walsh, at age forty-one, is Bob's son and Samantha's father. He's the anchor here in more ways than one. And, of course, the charming ten-year-old Samantha is a most compelling author and character.

To make it easy to keep track of who's storytelling at any given time, you'll find that person's name next to his or her written text. Sometimes we'll include a picture for emphasis. *Follow the Dog Home* covers the seventy-year time frame from 1941 to 2011. Some of us were not yet born, or were too young to remember each and every detail. So we relied upon historical accounts, photographs, old notes, and interviews with people who were familiar with our family stories. When the exact facts couldn't be uncovered, we made reasonable guesses based on the plausibility of what could have happened. We may not be 100 percent accurate at all times, but we're pretty close and we tried our best.

We live in a fast-paced ever-changing world in which the only constant is change. To keep up, men and women must reinvent themselves every couple of years. There's peace in posterity too, and often a pet in the middle. And when that pet is a dog, "it's heaven" as great grandfather Albert J. Walsh used to say.

ONE
Atwood Street

KEVIN WALSH

Life is good in Wellesley, Massachusetts. Always has been, always will be. We arrived in town the first week of August in 2009. My wife, Jean, and daughters Samantha and Amanda, and German Shepherd, Beverly, were looking for a fresh start after relocating from Wilmington, Delaware. I was starting a new job with a major television sports network after a year in limbo in a tough economy. After a few days of unpacking at our rental home on Francis Road near the Sprague Athletic Fields, we needed a break.

It was a Saturday morning and Beverly was eager to go for a walk. I needed to find a church for Mass the next day. A neighbor said St. Paul Church on Atwood Street was the closest one, and within walking distance. It was the perfect opportunity to take Beverly for her first long walk around town, get some exercise myself, and find a parish for the family.

Kevin Walsh. This is Kevin Walsh's second book. His first one, The Marrow in Me, *details his courageous journey to donate bone marrow to a sixteen-year-old boy he had never met. Kevin and his wife, Jean, have two daughters, Samantha and Amanda. He is a seasoned sports and news broadcaster with Comcast Sportsnet New England and New England Cable News Network. He was the lead reporter in the locker room when the Bruins won hockey's Stanley Cup in Vancouver in 2011. Turn on the tube; you might see Kevin looking right back at you.*

I put on my shorts, running shoes, and sweat-wicking shirt, and headed for the door. Beverly pawed at the door and wagged her tail so hard that it dented the venetian blinds! I clipped her pink leash onto her chain and off we went.

We walked down the driveway, turned right on Francis Road, and picked up the pace to a jog once we reached Worcester Street—better known as Route 9. We headed east on Route 9, south on Kingsbury, and over the train trestle where Kingsbury turns into State Street. Ten minutes into the run, Beverly and I turned right on Atwood Street.

It was a gorgeous summer morning, and I couldn't help but think: this is the perfect place for us. Located about thirteen miles west of downtown Boston, the Town of Wellesley, as it's officially called, resembles a Norman Rockwell painting. Its classic colonial and Victorian homes and streets are lined with old-fashioned lamps that light the way.

The earliest town history goes back to 1630. As written in Beth Hinchliffe's Wellesley historical authority—*Five Pounds Currency, Three Pounds of Corn*—the early pioneers paid that sum to Chiefs Nehoiden and Maugus for land along the Charles River. For the last century and a half, it's been home to one of the most beautiful suburbs in the world.

Three-year-old Beverly is the Walsh family's second German Shepherd. She loves to play with children and is especially happy to fetch the golf balls that Kevin chips around the backyard. When she's not outside playing ball, Beverly enjoys curling up in bed with older sisters Amanda and Samantha for a good read.

About the length of a par four, Atwood Street links State Street and Wellesley Avenue. It's the quintessential New England neighborhood that just about anyone would be proud to live in, and to which plenty aspire. The mostly colonial homes are above average in size and off the charts in charm. Traditional whites, grays, yellows, and greens dominate the home colors. Matching or contrasting louvered shutters accent the windows.

Everything fits. If you can imagine a well-dressed man or woman with accessories that complement a wristwatch, a belt, and a matching pair of shoes, you can imagine the good taste that Atwood Street has. The front-door light fixtures go well with the brass knockers and house numbers. Nothing is overdone, or underdone. It's just right. And it's been this way ever since the neighborhood was developed in the late 1920s.

Atwood Street may as well be Mayberry or Pleasantville. The difference is this is a real place, with really nice people who know their neighbors and like them. They do simple things—they play on the front lawn and sit on the stoop with their dogs. It's not because they don't have anywhere to go or nothing else to do; it's because there's no place they'd rather be.

Of course, when you have such an ideally perfect place, some people tend to resent it and derisively refer to the town in general as "Swellesley." But unlike the ultra-rich neighborhoods of Wellesley's other famous parts, the magic of Atwood Street is, if you work hard and do well, you just might make it here. You'll have to be very lucky with the timing, though, because the turnover only happens about every twenty years or so.

For those who left Atwood Street and are lucky enough to come back for a visit, the new neighbors welcome the old ones as if they had never left. Homecomings happen because there's a spirit that endures. Some returns are as simple as a knock on the door for one last look; others are much more involved.

There are still a few people living on Atwood Street who have been here since World War II. Many folks who moved out simply passed the house on to their children. So the family feel is still very much a part of the street. It has stood the test of time.

As I lumbered along Atwood Street that glorious August morning in 2009, the sweet smells of honeysuckle and morning glory flowers teased my nose. Sunlight broke through the trees and bounced off dewy plants. Sprinklers went tick, tick, tick, delivering the water that made the grass so green, the gardens so bright, and the driveways so wet. I could feel my heart rate increasing, sweat beading on my forehead, and a slight burn filling my thighs from the early jog. My first visit to Atwood Street was a good one, with just enough exertion to breathe hard, but not too much to be out of breath. The sync of my stride was in sync with the clink of Beverly's chain.

Ahead to the right was an opening in the trees. It was the back parking lot of St. Paul's Church. I'd be there in a moment, but not before taking in the scenery right in front of me and off to the sides. In a sweeping motion with the back of my right hand I wiped the sweat from my forehead and brow. When I tilted my head to the left to do it, my eye caught a stately house—not for the specifics—but the composite. The home colors were soft and similar, blending nicely with the trees and shrubs around it. It was stunning, as all-American as they come, the kind of house I'd love to buy.

A few moments later I turned into the driveway of St. Paul's, satisfied that the mission of finding the church was accomplished. But after looping around in the parking lot with Beverly and heading home, I felt thrown for a different kind of loop in an oddly special way. For a moment, I wondered whether I had seen that all-American house sometime before. Impossible, I thought. I had never set foot on Atwood Street until that day.

Those first few weeks, I took a lot of walks with Beverly—and not just for exercise. I was shopping for real estate. There's no better way to get a feel for a neighborhood than to walk it. So that's what I did, and Beverly couldn't have been happier. She's a tracker, constantly sniffing and often pulling me where she wants to go.

Beverly and I kept coming back to the neighborhood around St. Paul's. And when we did, Beverly took a particular liking to the smells of the properties around the halfway point of Atwood Street. I don't know why that was, it just … was. She would slow down and sniff, sometimes stopping abruptly. Whether this signified something greater, I did not know yet, but her sniffing certainly slowed me down and created the opportunity to take a closer look at the houses around her casting net.

Inevitably, my eyes would be drawn to the same beautiful home that caught my attention the first time, and so many other times since. There was a pull about the place—a connection. Beverly tugs me down that home's footpath almost every time we pass by on our regular walks now.

It turns out there's a very appropriate explanation for why she and I felt a strange pull at the house on Atwood Street for the first time in 2009.

I called my Aunt Jean (Walsh) Bryant. I learned a few weeks after moving to Wellesley that Aunt Jean had lived there for thirty-five years before retiring to Cape Cod in the late eighties. I figured if anyone might be able to explain the attraction, it would be Aunt Jean. Was the house on Atwood Street once hers?

"No, no, no," Aunt Jean answered. "We lived on Abbott Road. It was your father who lived on Atwood Street. You do know your family history in Wellesley don't you dee-ah?" Aunt Jean asked leadingly in her most loving of Boston accents.

Jean (Walsh) Bryant is the family historian. At age eighty-four, she remembers just about everything, which was instrumental in the amazing connection uncovered in this story. Even though she's my father's cousin, many of us call her "Aunt Jean."

Her answer shocked me. "No, actually I don't," I said, "other than your family living here."

"Your father lived on Atwood Street behind St. Paul's right before the war. He was just a baby when they moved out. He probably doesn't even remember it, dear."

When Aunt Jean shared the address of Dad's house, I was floored. It was the same house that Beverly sniffed around and made me do a double take.

While Aunt Jean was talking, my mind started drifting back in time. I wondered whether there were any photos of the old house. I remembered years ago that Dad had been cleaning out his basement in Ledyard, Connecticut. He sent me a dusty suitcase filled with old black and whites. I had looked at the pictures briefly before closing the suitcase up, not expecting to open it again for a while. My lasting memory—there's a lot of history in there that I don't understand—and I sure do look like my dad and grandfather when they were younger. Aunt Jean's voice snapped me back to our conversation.

.   .   .

"Is St. Paul's going to be your church?" Aunt Jean asked inquisitively.

Still shocked by the revelation I could hardly answer. "Yes, it will be," I managed to say a moment later.

"Well, great. When you get there, go to the back of the church and you'll see your grandfather's name on the back wall. He's on The Roll of Honor for having served in the war."

When we went to Mass the next Sunday, I walked through the stained oak doors that give St. Paul's additional character to its red bricks. To the left, I saw The Roll of Honor with names of dozens of parishioners who served in the World War and World War II. I looked to the bottom right and there it was, Albert J. Walsh, in gold letters looking right back at me. I was just two years old when he passed away in 1972.

To see your family name for the first time in a place of honor, and in the Lord's house, is a lot to handle. It is spiritual and profound—something you feel as much as you see. That visual evoked an internal validation that I had work to do beyond the original job that brought us to suburban Boston, and to Wellesley in particular.

In the fall of 2010, I started to put together the outline of this book with my dad and Samantha. I went through boxes, drawers, envelopes, you name it. When I got to Dad's dusty suitcase, one photo stopped me dead in my tracks. I saw my father as a child, posing with his family and his first dog Dee Dee on the stoop of a home. It looked so familiar. When I saw the house number above the door I knew why.

Bob Walsh (Kevin's dad), left, and his twin brother, Dick, as toddlers just months prior to Japan's attack on Pearl Harbor, sitting on the front stoop of the family home—on Atwood Street—with their dog Dee Dee, sister Boots, and mom. Albert Walsh (Bob's dad) would later join the war effort serving with the Navy

. . .

Just before Thanksgiving, I slipped a note inside the mail slot at the old family home on Atwood Street. I explained our family history there and asked if we could visit and re-create the family photo on the stoop, with new family additions and new dogs. A few days later, a nice email landed in my mailbox that said, "Sure."

Two weeks after the 2011 New Year, Dad and my stepmother Mary drove up to Massachusetts from

Connecticut. They brought their Corgi Annie with them. Jean and I brought our dog Beverly along with the girls to the house on Atwood Street. We shared bagels, blueberry breakfast cake, coffee, and warm conversation with our hosts. They couldn't have been more kind welcoming us in and sharing details of who lived in the house long after Dad's family left during World War II.

Before leaving, we plunked ourselves down on the stoop, trying our best to get the positioning of people and the angle of the shot just right. It wasn't easy. A blizzard had dumped almost two feet of snow on New England the day before, and temperatures that morning were in the single digits. Despite chattering teeth we tried to look happy and comfortable.

Just before we took the picture, the sun lifted over the oak trees lining the street, producing brilliant light, and bumping the temperature up just a smidge. It was perfect timing. The natural light, the glow in our hearts, and our gratitude for being welcomed home produced a warm, cheerful picture on the coldest of days. It was a magical way to bring my father back to his old home on Atwood Street seventy years later.

The Walsh family gathered on the stoop of the house on Atwood Street in January 2011, seventy years after Bob and his family lived there. From left: Beverly, Kevin, Bob holding Annie, Amanda, Jean, and Samantha.

I find it serendipitous that my family ended up in the same town where my father's family had earlier roots. Dad has no memory of it. Not because he's too old, but because he was too young. Jean and I had never been to Wellesley previously and had no preconceived desire to live there. We backed into the deal simply because Wellesley was the only town where we could find a rental home that would allow a dog as big as ours. Now that we're here, we love it and hope to stay forever.

When I look at the pictures of my dad sitting on the stoop of his Atwood Street home seventy years apart, I see a young boy who grew to become a distinguished, elderly man. I see the changing seasons and changing fashions. I see those who have left us and those who have joined us. But more than anything, I see a constant, a common ground—dogs linking the generations together like nothing else can.

Our dogs have given us so much: lessons to learn, challenges to face, pain to bear, and joy to share. If they hadn't come in the order that they did, with the timing of their arrivals and departures what they were, what's become of our lives might be very different. Looking back, without our need for a rental home that allowed a big dog, and without Beverly's curious nose, there would have been no Wellesley for us, no return to Atwood Street for Dad, and no story to be told. It's that simple: we followed the dog home.

TWO

First Dog, Second World War, a Family Torn

BOB WALSH

I'm not sure what my father's early history was with dogs, whether he had them growing up. He very well may have, I don't know. My sister, Boots, says they first had a Boston Terrier—but that was before I was born. I just know we always had dogs in our house.

My first dog was Dee Dee. Dee Dee was short for her registered name of Dimity Davis. Everybody had a nickname back then, even the dogs. Perhaps readers can remember their very first dog and what that dog meant to them. Dee Dee was a Smooth Fox Terrier mix. She was a somewhat scruffy and very energetic little pup with an enormous self-image. She was a little-bit-of-a-thing with a great heart and huge appetite, which would eventually be her undoing.

Bob Walsh. For almost forty years, Bob Walsh worked in the pharmaceutical industry before retiring to live the good life in his early sixties. That means spending time with his second wife, Mary. Bob married Mary in 1995. She too was a widow who had lost her spouse. Their extended Brady Bunch family includes nine adult children and twenty grandchildren. Regularly by Bob's side is his ever faithful dog, a Corgi named Annie. Whether Bob is building a fly rod from scratch, tying flies, or four-wheeling into a fishing hole filled with trout, Annie is often with him.

Dee Dee was rarely far away from my twin brother and me, unless of course she was foraging for food. She was affectionate if you entered her space, but more often than not, she preferred to lie down a step or two away.

Marie Beth (Walsh) Hall—we call her Boots or Booty— Bob's older sister at age seventy-eight, also is a writer and family historian.

"Oh, Dee Dee would often keep an eye on the twins. She wouldn't get too close, but if you put a barrier in the way, she'd get very upset," my sister Marie Beth (Boots) Hall says. "Right around dinner was the crying hour. The twins would fight. They were hungry and grumpy and would sometimes take it out on each other. My mother had them fenced in, inside of a playroom just off the kitchen. Dee Dee was on the outside. She would cry, whine, and howl with them. I think the twins' crying hurt Dee Dee's ears. And she didn't want to be separated from the kids."

I was too young to remember those moments—or even that photo of us with Dee Dee on the front stoop of the house on Atwood Street—but that's nice to hear now. Not the crying tales—but the part about how much Dee Dee loved us. We certainly loved her. Dee Dee had the run of the house—as long as it was downstairs. My mother didn't think dogs should be on beds or upstairs. The upstairs was for people and sleeping. Outside, though, it was free rein, and Dee Dee would follow her nose to wherever she could get a free meal.

"She was a bum," Boots says, "and she would go from house to house where people would feed her. Sometimes she was gone for a couple of days at a time. We never really worried about it. She always came back and was never hungry."

If we decided to search for her, though, it didn't take much more than walking down our street and calling out her name. "Dee Dee, Dee Dee," was often followed by the

Samantha *told Bob "Grandpops": "Sometimes my dad tells Beverly to jump up on our beds to wake us up in the morning."*

Bob "Grandpops": *"Really? What does she do?"*

Amanda *(giggling): "She sticks her nose in my ear and licks my face! Did your dogs ever do that to you when you were a boy?"*

Bob "Grandpops": *"No. My mother—your great grandmother— never allowed dogs on the bed."*

sound of a front door opening and a voice calling out, "She's over here."

To understand how much Dee Dee meant to me, you have to have an understanding of what life was like in my family and America at the time. Life was good. The nation was just about over the Great Depression, and my dad had a good job in the fast growing telephone industry. We moved from New Jersey to Wellesley in 1940. It was practically a homecoming for Dad who was born and raised in the nearby Forest Hills section of Boston's Jamaica Plain.

I look back at old photos and see an age of innocence, when we did simple things like take a bath in a tin washtub in the backyard with my dog Dee Dee ever watchful. What fun we didn't find in the backyard we found at Morses Pond near Wellesley College.

Bob and Dick Walsh splash in a washtub in the family backyard on Atwood Street, 1941. Dee Dee in the background keeps a close watch.

Baseball was in its Golden Age, too. Up and down Atwood Street and across America, you could hear radios crackling with the call. The Red Sox were king in New England and Ted Williams was God. But God got robbed in 1941. Despite hitting .406, Ted Williams lost the MVP to Joe DiMaggio and his fifty-six-game hitting streak.

Even with grumblings about Williams's lost award during neighborhood stickball games, there was a healthy respect for Joe DiMaggio on Atwood Street. There were plenty of New York transplants around us who rooted for the Yankees, or the Brooklyn Dodgers. Plus, Joe's younger brother, Dominic, a seven-time All-Star, played center field for the Red Sox. Before Sunday afternoon games at Fenway Park, you could catch "Dom" DiMaggio at morning Mass at St. Paul's in Wellesley. The Yankees won the World Series in 1941, and the Red Sox finished second in the American League. Still, it was a very good year—until December.

Everything changed on December 7, 1941. The Japanese attacked Pearl Harbor, sending shock waves across the globe, the U.S. mainland, and certainly down Atwood Street. For my dad and a lot of men, the attack stirred something inside. Dad wanted to do something about it. Eventually he did, with ramifications that would affect us all. My older sister remembers Dad becoming very quiet

Bob's dad, Albert J. Walsh, introduced the Walsh family to dogs. He raised five dogs including Dee Dee, Frisky, Poker, Fly Boy, and Claudia.

after Pearl Harbor and having discussions with my mom about what he was going to do.

We're pretty sure the unfortunate circumstances of the war gave Dad a chance to fulfill what, for him, was unfinished business. Dad went to the United States Naval Academy and graduated in 1924. Most men who went to the service academies back then were expected to make a career out of the military. But while at Annapolis, Dad's eyes deteriorated. It didn't affect his studies, but it would have a lasting impact on his military career. His poor eyesight meant he couldn't serve on warships. That essentially put the kibosh on Navy upward mobility. With his career advancement limited, Dad was given the option to resign from active duty and join the Reserves upon graduation. That is what he did.

After a few months of cooling his heels and successfully playing cards with his friends, Dad joined his dad at the phone company. The telephone industry was our family business and nearly everyone else's back then. Grandpa (Daniel Walsh) got Dad the job. That was how things worked.

Dad's return to active duty during the war came with a caveat. His job in communications at AT&T was considered "essential" to the war effort. His superiors didn't quite understand why he thought he could better serve his country in a capacity different from what he was already doing. Clearly, Dad wanted more.

In the spring of 1942, Dad left for the Navy. It was a sad time for us, but we were very proud of him. He still couldn't be on a warship because of his eyes, so he was assigned to Solomons Island, Maryland, the initial base for training crews in amphibious operations. The training at Solomons Island and at the U.S. Naval Amphibious Base in Little Creek, Virginia—where Dad later served—would play pivotal roles in the amphibious assaults in places like Normandy. When his work was done in the Mid-Atlantic region, he would later serve in Hawaii.

The Walsh Family, 1944:
Back row: Albert, Jr., and Marie Beth "Boots"
Front row: Bob, Elizabeth, and Dick

Joining the war effort was a family affair filled with upheaval and uprooting. When Dad left, we moved from Wellesley to Providence, Rhode Island. We moved in with Momma and Poppa MacAdam, my maternal grandparents. It was especially tough on my older siblings because they had to change schools. That's never easy on anyone. While the rest of us missed our dad and worried about our future, Dee Dee was in doggie heaven in the home on the one hundred block of Benefit Street near Brown University. Poppa Mac doted on that dog and took her everywhere he went, including to work.

Poppa Mac was a tough Scotsman who smoked sweet-smelling tobacco in a pipe. If you were looking for him, you could just follow your nose. Or you could call out Dee Dee's name and retrace her steps. She would lead you to him because she was always with him. When he left for work as a night watchman at the Walsh-Kaiser Shipyard, Dee Dee walked with him. She'd stay at the shipyard for a while before walking back home, arriving promptly each night at eleven.

Summer came and Dick and I were sent to Durham, New Hampshire, for an extended stay with my Uncle John and Aunt Vera Neville at the University of New Hampshire. My mother and older siblings spent the summer in Little Creek, Virginia, where my father had been transferred to be the first Executive Officer of the new Amphibious Training Station.

When summer was over, minus Dad, the family reunited. We lived for a year in a rented home in Edgewood, Rhode Island, before moving on to a house mom bought on Cornell Avenue in the Gaspee Plateau section of Warwick, Rhode Island.

It's hard to keep track of it all. Were it not for my older sister Boots, I probably couldn't tell you much about the early life we lived. By any measure, it was a vagabond life. We were moving all the time.

By the time the summer of 1943 rolled in, we were badly in need of a vacation. As much as the war was pulling us apart, it actually helped pull us together for the course of a couple of months. We unwound from the stress of life with a summer-long family vacation to Cape Cod. Mom called the Cape "heaven," and with an opportunity that really did seem heaven-sent, we lucked into a house rental in charming Falmouth Heights.

We stayed at the Bristol family compound. The Bristols were wealthy people who built a handful of homes for their adult children on a compound. One of the families had a father away at war and chose not to spend the summer at the compound. That made the home available to us. A summer on the Cape in one of the Bristol homes: it really didn't get much better than that.

Our home for the summer was a classic wood shake Cape Cod–style home with four bedrooms. My mom had her own room. So did Boots, and my older brother, Al. I shared a room with Dick. That's how it always was. As twins, we shared everything. There was a green screened-in porch that sat a couple of feet above the ground. Dee

Dee spent a lot of time under that porch and would later regret it.

The Bristols were lovely people who made us feel very welcome. They treated us like family and told us to use the property however we wished. There was a tennis court. My brother Al was an excellent player, but my sister suggests he may have been more interested in who was hanging around the court than in serve and volley. Betsy Bristol was an attractive gal who caught Al's attention. We were not sure what became of it, and even if we were, we probably wouldn't tell.

When Al wasn't flirting with Betsy, he and Boots were diving off Falmouth Heights Pier and swimming a grand distance over to the main beach. Dick and I would catch up with them later on the sand. Mom just sat in her chair, watching us and relaxing in the warm sun. Back at the compound Dee Dee was romping in a salt marsh, raising more hell digging for the crabs and clams than a heron ever could. Unfortunately, she found another place to dig.

Underneath the porch, Dee Dee found the home of a burrowing animal. Determined to get a better look at what was living in the underground den, Dee Dee made it her mission to dig the existing hole deeper and wider. After a furious spurt of energy that sprayed a rooster tail of dirt, a tail of another kind lifted and sprayed something else.

"OOOOwwwwwwwwwwwww!" came the awful sound of Dee Dee's dog voice.

It was more of a cry than a bark, and it was clear she was in trouble. We heard her cries for help and rushed to the door. Dee Dee came trudging up the steps of the porch with her ears peeled back, her head down, and her tail between her legs. She had yellowish spots all about her face, in the corners of her eyes, and extending down her back. Her eyes were watering and her nose was running. And the smell, THE SMELL, was unmistakably the pungent smell of skunk musk.

"Oh, I remember it well," Boots says, "poor Dee Dee was so embarrassed. How bad did it smell? You know how bad it is when you smell a skunk that's been hit by a car? I would say it's easily five times as bad."

If your dog has never been sprayed by a skunk, consider yourself among the fortunate. The cleanup is among the dirtiest jobs you could ever have. The smell goes without saying. But it's more than that. The vapors from the musk irritate your eyes and throat too.

Mom acted fast. She got in the car, drove to the country store and bought out the store's supply of tomato juice. She came back and filled up a tin washtub. She lifted Dee Dee into the tub, trying to stay calm so the dog would too. Dee Dee totally submitted. With a towel, Mom dabbed at the oily dots of musk sitting on top of the dog's fur. She was careful not to press too hard and move her hand in a windshield wiper motion, as that would only press the oil deeper into the coat and make the smell last longer. One cleaning wasn't enough. Neither was a second. After the third scrubbing, we thought we had the smell wiped out.

Dee Dee, a Smooth Fox Terrier mix, was Bob Walsh's first dog, 1941. Dee Dee would often wander and beg for food. Her trust in strangers who fed her would ultimately be her undoing. The cause of Dee Dee's death was a great mystery for many years, but was finally revealed in shocking fashion to Bob Walsh in 2011.

Feeling better about ourselves and Dee Dee, we dumped what was left in the washtub down by the marsh. Dee Dee followed us down for a look. When we came back to the house and bounded back up the steps and into the house, Dee Dee stopped dead in her tracks at the door.

"Come on, Dee Dee. Come on in," my mom called as we went back into the house.

Dee Dee wouldn't budge. We didn't understand. Dee Dee always wanted to be with us and would go to great lengths to do it. Then we figured it out. Our imperfect human noses couldn't smell what she did. She still smelled herself and was too embarrassed to come inside. We tried to drag her in by the collar, but she dug her claws into the wood floor. She would stay outside on the porch for a week. And then on the eighth day, she came walking right in as if nothing happened. It took that long for the most sensitive of noses to know the stench was gone.

When summer ended, we returned to our new home on Cornell Avenue in Warwick, Rhode Island, where we lived for a year. We still made frequent trips to Momma and Poppa Mac's in Providence, and Dee Dee always came along. Dee Dee and Poppa Mac got back into their familiar routine, walking together to the shipyard.

When we weren't visiting my grandparents, Dick and I spent a lot of time playing with Dee Dee on the lawn of our new home on Cornell Avenue. Our new neighbors noticed us and most were quick with kindness. Dee Dee, ever the beggar, found new folks to feed her. And if they weren't willing, she'd help herself to whatever was in their trash cans.

One neighbor, an elderly man who lived diagonally across the street watched us regularly from a distance. He had evil in his eyes and darkness in his heart. It wasn't just us. He hated all of the neighbors and their dogs. He was quick to scold when balls bounced near his property. He also chased dogs away with a bark of his own and a jab with his cane. The old codger wasn't just cruel, he was crafty.

On a particular day we saw Dee Dee over on his property munching away on food that had clearly been left for her. Dee Dee never returned. A few days later, my mother and sister went looking for her. They came home looking as if they had seen a ghost. I asked what was wrong, but they said nothing. Later Mom said Dee Dee had gone to visit Momma and Poppa Mac, but never made it back to the house on Benefit Street after seeing Poppa Mac off to work. It was all so mysterious.

Dick and I were very sad. Our third wheel was gone and we missed Dee Dee terribly. We speculated amongst ourselves that she might have been kidnapped, or run over by a truck.

"That's not what happened," Boots reveals sixty-five years later, "she was poisoned. That evil man across the street poisoned her. We found her body in an empty lot about three houses away. There was a trail of vomit that led right to the old man's house and what was left of the poisoned meat."

Hearing the revelation floored me. If we knew what happened and had clear evidence with poisoned meat and an unapologetic man grinning back at us, why didn't we tell the police about it?

"Because there was so much going on back then with the war," Boots says, "people were busy just trying to get through the day and often without fathers and husbands around."

As tough as losing Dee Dee was on me, it hardly compared with losing my best friend in the world. That would come several months later under different, but similar, circumstances. The vehicle that drove our family loss came unexpectedly. There is never a good time for the kind of news I'm about to share, and it came at a time in our family when we were finally together again.

Yes we moved again, but this time it was a move that brought us all together once more. In early 1945, Dad came home from Hawaii. He had been gone a total of almost three years. Housing was available to us on base in Portsmouth, Virginia, at the Naval Shipyard.

The mood on base was cautiously optimistic. By late July and early August the war was coming to a head. For six months the United States had made use of intense strategic fire-bombing of sixty-seven Japanese cities. Plenty of people wondered whether the war might soon end. While military wives had those conversations over coffee, Dick and I focused on what mattered most to us— getting ourselves into that big swimming pool on base as often as we could.

Bob and Dick Walsh with Dee Dee in the background, circa 1941

Suddenly, Dick fell ill. He had what in today's world we'd generally classify as flu-like symptoms—fever, abdominal pain, joint inflammation, and a stiff neck. At first doctors thought it was Cat Scratch Fever, but polio was prevalent at the time and it was impossible not to think about who and where it might strike next.

Shortly after the atomic bombs were dropped on Hiroshima and Nagasaki, the Japanese surrendered on August 15, 1945. Victory over Japan Day, or V-J Day, sparked instant parties all around us. But we didn't feel like celebrating. That same day, five-year-old Dick was diagnosed with a severe case of polio. The news was devastating.

Soon after Dick's diagnosis, the family split up again. In the fall of 1945, my parents took Dick to the Roosevelt Warm Springs Institute for Rehabilitation in Georgia where he would be treated for a year. My brother Al and sister Boots went back to Providence to live with Momma and Poppa Mac on Benefit Street. I went to live with my father's folks in Jamaica Plain, not far from the Forest Hills T-stop.

People ask me the typical twin questions about whether I felt a part of me was lost, or guilty that my twin was ill instead of me. I honestly can't say I did to either question, or I just wasn't old enough to understand those feelings. But I do know this, I missed my brother. He was my best friend. I never had to look for someone to play with because Dick was always there and ready to play too.

Polio took all that and him away. It was my second big loss in a relatively short amount of time. First Dee Dee, and now Dick was undergoing treatment for a long stretch.

THREE

A Dog That Hit the Jackpot

BOB

Our family had gone through a dog-less stretch of more than a year because of our unsettled family life with the war and Dick's treatment for polio. After getting Dick settled in down in Georgia, my parents came back north. Dad went back to work with the phone company, but he was transferred to New York City. Another move! In 1946, we landed in Montclair, New Jersey.

We lived on the one hundred block of Essex Avenue. It was a four-bedroom gray colonial with dark gray shutters and window boxes for flowers. It was the perfect location. We were just a block away from Edgemont Elementary School and a short walk to the Watchung Avenue train station for Dad's commute into Manhattan.

We were finally in a home that was ours, and we started to talk about getting another dog. Based on a collection of family memories, it was thought a dog would do us—and especially me—some good. We were the new people in the neighborhood. It would be several more months before Dicky got out of the hospital and making new friends in a new place wasn't easy.

The thought of a new dog sounded great, but the reality was that money was very tight. Dick's treatment at Warm Springs was very expensive, about $50 a day. That's the equivalent of about $600 a day in today's economy. Dad was a proud man and would not accept any money from the Sister Kenny Fund that provided funding for the treatment of polio. There was no medical insurance back then either, so the cost was entirely out of my parents' pocket. There was just no leftover money for nonessential purchases.

Someone suggested picking up a dog at the pound. We gave it a shot and brought home Frisky. Frisky was a mid-sized mongrel who really did live up to his name. He was frisky and he loved to run. If he got out of the house or off his leash, forget it! It took forever to corral him. One day, he disappeared for hours. Eventually, we found him waiting to be discovered under a street sign that read Essex Avenue in Maplewood. It may be a few towns over and eight miles away, but my dog could read!

As much as we loved the idea of having a dog back in the house, the truth is Frisky was a tough dog to love. His wanderlust became a lot of work, and his behavior was a liability. All these years later, I still feel bad for the trash man. As if picking up the trash at six o'clock in the morning wasn't hard enough already, that poor guy had to use the can's lid for a shield whenever Frisky sought to hem his pants.

In 1947, Dick came home from Warm Springs, Georgia. He brought back a cheerful spirit and warm Southern drawl that he picked up while completing first grade in the hospital. I was just so happy to have my best friend and twin back. I had somebody to join me for The Green Hornet radio show. We chatted a lot and I brought Dick up to speed on just about everything he missed while he was gone. I also had a pal to walk to second grade with— which is really saying something considering how badly polio had damaged Dick's legs.

Doctors thought Dick would never be able to walk again. The fact that he could was really a testament to his indomitable spirit and sense of humor. He also learned to dance at Mrs. Stautinger's Dance Class, to ride a bike, to fight, and eventually marry and have three children.

Our dog, Frisky, was as happy as he'd ever been. With Dick back in the fold, Frisky probably saw my brother as another littermate—someone to play with. There's just something about dogs and children. Sometimes that playfulness was a bit much as Frisky seemed to do everything big. Frisky saw no foul in bouncing up to Dick's face. With Dick's disability, that led to some tumbles. We kids suspected that Frisky might not last. Mom and Dad made it clear: Frisky was going back to the pound.

Even if Frisky wasn't a comfortable fit for the family, there's an instant discomfort when you take a dog away. Crazy dogs bring something important to the party too. Be it sound, spirit, a presence, whatever; when they're gone, there's a void. We felt it, but in many ways, we felt helpless to do something about it because of the family's financial situation.

Not wanting to try a pound puppy again, Dad must have been cooking something up in his head. He missed having a dog in the house too. Then, one day in 1948, without any heads up, Dad came home with a small dog under his arm. It was a Cocker Spaniel with a tan coat. Dad named him Dealer's Choice. Apparently there had been a successful night of Dealer's Choice Poker, and Dad walked away with $50 in winnings from his card play. He used the money to buy a dog, which we affectionately called Poker.

Poker was a great dog and really Dad's dog more than anyone else's. Dad had a red leather chair where he read the newspaper and enjoyed a smoke. Nobody else was allowed to sit in that chair, but Poker could. When Dad was gone, Poker was all ours. He loved to play. I would take him out back and throw the ball, which he dutifully retrieved. But often his attention was divided. There was a cat named Smokey who lived next door. He loved to taunt Poker.

Smokey looked like his name. He had a smoke-colored gray coat and bright yellow eyes. He had a way about him that let you know he was looking at you. You could feel his eyes on you, turn around and there he was looking you right in the eye with a bold gold stare. I kind of admired his gumption, but Poker wanted nothing more than to get at that cat.

Smokey would come over when the coast was clear, sprinkle a couple of drops of tinkle on our grass, and later watch Poker have fits following his nose. Smokey's scent would lead to his back door, and Poker would follow the trail with smoke coming out of his floppy ears. When Poker got to the back steps, he'd look up with jowls jiggling and teeth bared. Smokey only fueled the fire by grinning back smugly from the safe side of the window's glass.

"Some day. Some day you'll get him," I told Poker over and over again when it was time to bring him back inside.

Poker loved to be fussed over. When Dad would sit in his leather chair, Poker would come right over and prop his head up for petting. With a gentle touch Dad would stroke the dog from the top of his head and down his back. Dad would do it until his arm got tired, or Poker would collapse and fall asleep from the hypnotic repetition.

As much as Poker would strike a pose next to my father's chair for the love and attention Dad gave him, he would do the same for me, as I dabbled in art. Poker would sit at attention for almost an hour as I sketched his headshot and bust on a pad. I think his obedience came from the fact that I would praise him for sitting so still. I would talk to him about things going on at school and in the neighborhood as I waved the pencil across the pad. The end result was something I felt really good about. Also, I remember the connection we had as much as the art. We were real pals.

Poker was there for me when my brother Dick and others weren't available. Dick had to do a lot of physical therapy because of the polio. Mom would help him with that, or simply rub his sore legs.

"With Mom taking care of Dicky, and Al and I being older and doing our own thing, Bob would sometimes get the shaft and be lonely," my sister Boots remembers, "so, that's why I think Bob really bonded with Poker."

I was also taking on more responsibility with the dog's care. Mom and Dad did the heavy lifting, but it was expected the kids would feed the dog when told, or whenever Poker indicated he was hungry by putting his paw on my leg and letting out a little whimper.

In 1949, we were in fourth grade. We were ten years old. There was an incident involving a fellow fourth grader who was quite large for his age. I vividly remember the big kid taunting Dicky about his limp and leg brace. He called Dicky a cripple. It was the kind of thing that would bring a lot of kids to tears, but not Dicky and not me. I was mad and determined to get even.

I took off running after the kid. Another friend joined me. I think the offending boy was surprised how quickly we caught up to him. He hadn't even reached the corner before we grabbed him. He put up a little fight but was totally overmatched. We dragged him by his wrists and shoulders all the way back to Dicky, who was grinning and waiting. Dicky's eyes lit up when his tormentor approached with a fearful look on his face. Dick dropped his crutches, reached out with his arms and said, "Let him go."

As soon as we turned him over, Dick had the kid wrapped up in a tight bear hug. The kid tried to wiggle away but was no match for Dick's unbelievable upper-body strength. Although just a fourth grader, Dick was probably as strong as a high school offensive lineman because of his time on crutches. Pleading for mercy, the big kid was in tears and out of breath.

After about a minute, Dick dropped him. He had all but squeezed the life out of him. The much larger boy walked away, looking small and defeated.

A short time later, there was a knock at the door. My mother answered. A woman with the same ten-year-old boy standing alongside asked if there was a boy named Bobby Walsh who lived there. "Yes, I have a son named Bobby," Mom answered. "Why do you want to know?"

"Well a boy named Bobby beat up my son," she said.

She left out the part about Dick being teased, or maybe her son didn't tell her about it. Dick and I could hear the conversation from where we were in the kitchen. We made our way over to the breezeway for a better listen, but we were careful not to stick our heads out too far so as not to be noticed.

As the volume and tone of the conversation grew, so did Dick's eyes. He looked at me with a sense of shock and wonder about whether we might be in trouble. No sooner did I shrug my shoulders, Mom called out my name, summoning me to the front door.

I left Dicky and Poker in the kitchen. Mom pointed at the boy and asked me, "Did you beat that boy up?"

"Yes," I answered.

"Why did you do that?" Mom wanted to know, somewhat angry herself now.

"Because he called Dicky a cripple," I announced.

As soon as I said it, Dick came hobbling to the front door with Poker in tow for moral support. Boots caught ear of it and followed. Poker poked his head out from between Mom's legs and barked at the boy. The other mother was mortified by what she saw and what her son had said.

"She grabbed her son by the ear and started hitting him on the back of the head with her purse," Boots remembers with a laugh. "She was whacking him all the way down the street."

That boy didn't dare tease Dicky again. Recently my son Kevin, ever the reporter, put the squeeze on me for more information. "So who was the kid that Uncle Dick squeezed?"

"I'm not telling," I told him.

In addition to feeding Poker, I also tried to take on his grooming requirements too. Cutting a Cocker's coat is no easy task. I tried and tried and tried. I'm not sure how handsome he looked when I was done with him, but his hair was definitely shorter. I don't think he was into appearances anyway.

As blessed as we were to have Poker, he was not blessed with longevity. He lived to be just six years old. He fell ill one day in 1953, and Dad took him away. About a half-hour later we heard Dad's car pull into the driveway. I walked over to the dining room window and looked outside. Dad was sitting in front of the steering wheel cupping his forehead with his hand. He sat there for a few minutes, squeezing his thumb and fingers together as if to rub out a headache. I just stared out the window wondering what was taking him so long to get out.

"What's your father doing?" my mom asked, seeing me from across the room.

"I don't know," I told her.

Almost as soon as I said that I saw my dad reaching for something in the front passenger seat. I thought he was reaching for Poker, but the back of the front seat was too high to see down to the seat itself. When he got out of the car, he had Poker's leash and collar in his right hand, but no dog. He walked up the steps slowly, opened the door, and came inside. He took his long overcoat off even slower, while still holding the dog's leash and collar. He got stuck in the sleeves, but eventually wiggled his way out. There was a growing sense of unease that we all felt.

In a tossing motion, Dad's keys landed on a small table by the kitchen with a thud and a jingle. We could hear his footsteps on the hardwood as he walked toward the front room where we had all gathered. When he got to the front room, he looked at us kids and my mother and then down at his hands, which held the dog's essentials. He looked so sad.

Finally he looked up and simply said, "Poker died."

Nobody said a word. It was clear Dad was upset and any questions would only make him feel worse. "I think Dad took Poker's death especially hard because it was the first dog that was truly his," my sister remembers.

I just remember feeling really sad too. I was sad for my dad and sad for me. Little did I know a few years later that Dad and I would share another loss and connect on a deeper level. History would repeat itself thirty-four years later, only this time with me as a father and my son Kevin.

Oh yeah, one other thing about Poker. Not even an hour or so after Poker's death, Smokey the Cat made a visit to our house. He sat on a table in our backyard with the confidence of a cock in a henhouse. He knew Poker was dead and had the audacity to rub it in. I never did like that cat.

FOUR

Fly Boy
and the Grave Digger

BOB

It was 1954, and I was fourteen. Following Poker's death, we went about a year without a dog. If you ask me, it was a year too long. I just missed the friendship and the familiarity of chains jingling and all the other joys that a dog brings. An unfortunate health scare involving old family friends ultimately became our benefit.

My Aunt Vera Neville had known the Phillipson family for years. They were veterinarians. When they weren't busy healing sick animals, they bred prized Cocker Spaniels and Miniature (Tea Cup) Poodles. Their kennel was called Philsworth. It was located on Cape Cod.

The Phillipsons were lovely people, and we visited them as often as we could. A few years prior, when I was ten, Mrs. Phillipson taught me a very valuable lesson about a love for animals that I've never forgotten. One day, while visiting her, I went on a fishing excursion. I returned with a bountiful catch. I was very proud of the dozen blackfish hanging off the stringer I had draped over my shoulder.

"What are you going to do with those?" Mrs. Phillipson asked.

"I don't know," I answered.

"Well we never kill an animal unless we're going to eat it," she responded.

So she proceeded to debone and fry the fish I had caught. It was rough on the eyes and nose, and the taste was even worse. Lesson learned. Despite a lifetime and love of fishing since then, I've never purposely killed a fish. And my appreciation for life extends beyond the sea.

Mrs. Phillipson suffered a heart attack in 1954, and, at the advice of her doctor, she gave up the breeding business. No longer able to care for her dogs, Mrs. Phillipson was looking for families who would take care of them. Not only did we take in one of her prized animals, we would eventually take two and help two other families in our neighborhood to do the same.

I remember traveling to the Cape to pick up Fly Boy. He was three or four years old when we got him. He was a black-and-white Cocker Spaniel. I don't know why he was named Fly Boy, but he would leap and crash to earth regularly and spectacularly! My dad built Fly Boy a pen out back by the garage. The fence was about three feet high. It didn't take us long to figure out that Fly Boy had impressive leaping ability. Instead of waiting for us to unlatch the gate, he'd do us the favor of jumping into his pen. He hurdled that fence with plenty of room to spare and enjoyed the praise he got for doing it.

Fly Boy, however, didn't like to stay inside the pen once we left. So he made brave attempts to jump out. He always came up short, which didn't make sense because the ground was level on each side. If he could jump in with ease, he could certainly jump out. Only he couldn't, and he just about impaled himself every time he tried. There's no other reasonable explanation other than he must have had a psychological barrier.

Fly Boy's mental block would prove to test the mental health of us and the neighbors. He would howl and howl and howl some more. Eventually, he found another way out. He dug under the fence. We just couldn't win with that dog.

Fly Boy's howling wasn't limited to the outdoors. He did it inside too. It was so bad that we had to put him inside the cellar at bedtime. Even then you could still hear him all the way upstairs, which made for plenty of sleepless nights.

Because the dog had been given to us so graciously from the Phillipsons, we had to make it work. But the howling was becoming too much to bear. Repetitive sound is a proven form of psychological torture. Believe me, we were losing our minds. How did we fix it? We added another dog, courtesy of the Phillipsons.

Claudia was another black-and-white Cocker. She was a couple of years older than Fly Boy and an absolute doll. When we went to pick her up at the Philsworth Kennel, she approached me with something in her mouth. It was a rock.

"Why does she chew rocks?" I asked Dr. Phillipson.

"She doesn't chew them. She just carries them around in her mouth," Dr. Phillipson answered.

When we got her back to North Jersey, I made sure that she would always have a ball in her mouth. She was such a love. Whenever I came home from school, or ventured out to the backyard to play, she always grabbed a ball and brought it over to play fetch. She was attentive and so eager to please.

Claudia couldn't have been more different from Fly Boy. She was like day, he was like night. She was much calmer, and it was our hope that she might settle down the naughty boy. Fly Boy still howled with Claudia around, but much less than before. She was saintly in her tolerance of his howling and other peculiarities. It was almost as

Cocker Spaniels Fly Boy and Claudia were from the same breeder, but were as different as two dogs can be. He was a chronic howler who would often take flight while trying to escape his pen. He could jump into it, but not out of it. Go figure. Claudia, on the other hand, was a doll and a foil for Fly Boy. One morning, Claudia started digging a massive hole in the backyard. Never a digger before, we wondered why. When we found her in the hole later in the afternoon, we understood.

if she knew her job was to tame him. The result wasn't perfect, but the effort was heroic.

Claudia was spayed and Fly Boy was neutered. That kept them from multiplying. One Fly Boy was enough. Another Claudia would have been lovely, but that was not in the cards. The dogs did everything together.

One day in 1956, I looked out the window and noticed Fly Boy moving toward his pen with his right side dragging along. He had suffered a massive stroke and could hardly walk. His attempts to jump into his kennel, just like he had always done before, were even more heartbreaking. He was brought to the vet that same day and was put down.

Samantha, Kevin, and Bob talking about Fly Boy, 2011

Samantha: *"Grandpops, could Fly Boy really fly?"*

Bob "Grandpops": *"No, but he thought he could."*

Samantha: *"What do you mean?"*

Bob "Grandpops": *"Well maybe he could fly—a little. He just had troubling landing, and often ended up bouncing off the rail of his pen."*

It's a good thing Fly Boy died before Claudia. Had it been the other way around, he would have been inconsolable. As much as Fly Boy's passing may have been a blessing to us, Claudia took his loss hard. He was her pal and her job. So his death was a double loss to her. People who have two dogs know what I'm talking about.

A couple of years after Fly Boy flew to heaven, Claudia was digging furiously in the backyard. The effort was almost cartoonish in intensity, with dirt flying everywhere and Claudia hell-bent on unearthing more earth.

"What's with Claudia digging out back?" my mom wanted to know.

"I don't know," I answered, "she's just digging."

After finishing lunch, I went back to the spot behind a small bush where Claudia was on her way to China. Her black nose had turned brown from a collection of loose soil that stuck to it. She didn't want to be bothered. I went back into the house and did some chores.

After a half-hour or so, I went to check on Claudia. I looked out the back window and didn't see her. I opened the door and called her name. No response. So I went to the back part of our property where I last saw her digging behind the bush. As I approached I could see the pile of dirt was noticeably bigger. Then I reached the hole. Claudia was curled up inside.

"Claudia! Claudia!" I called.

She didn't answer. I knew she was gone. My dog had dug her own grave. She must have known something was wrong and wanted to die alone with dignity. I had lost dogs before, but this was the first time I had actually seen one dead. I was very sad and went inside to tell my mother. She immediately called my dad.

When Dad came home, we walked back to the gravesite together. He just stared at Claudia for a moment and said nothing. Dad wasn't a man to show much outward emotion, but his pause said plenty. Seeing Claudia in the hole left a hole in his heart too. He took a deep breath and lifted Claudia out, placing her gently on the ground next to the hole.

For a moment Dad looked around wondering what to do. Then he turned and headed for the garage. He returned wearing work gloves and carrying a rounded shovel. He stuck the pointy part of the shovel into the hole and jumped on the flat edges of the back, plunging it deeper into the soil. He lifted the loosened dirt and put it on the pile that Claudia had made by herself.

Dad dug in silence until the hole was twice the size and the appropriate depth for burial. He wrapped Claudia in a blanket, placed her at the bottom of the grave, and covered her with dirt. He did the heavy lifting, but he wasn't alone.

I was with him. We didn't speak because we didn't have to. Our beloved dog was a bridge connecting us in heart and spirit. It was not what either of us wanted, but it was a moment I'll never forget, not only for the loss, but also for that moment of bonding with Dad.

To the best of our knowledge Claudia remains right where she always wanted to be: at home.

FIVE

New Family, New Dog, Murphy Gone Mad

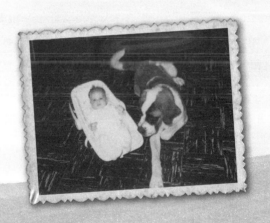

BOB

I had always had a fascination with big dogs, but never owned one myself. After graduating from Georgetown, I spent three years in the Air Force, stationed in Kansas City, Missouri, as an intelligence briefing officer. A fellow officer had a German Shepherd. That dog was an extension of him. We'd walk to the Bachelor Officers' Quarters and the dog would come with us, walking about twenty feet to his left. It was a striking sight. They were clearly a team.

After finishing up my three-year active duty commitment in the service, I had plans of starting my own team with people and pets. I proposed marriage to Carole Hynes, a nursing student, whom I'd met on a blind date in New York City seven years prior. She accepted! Carole, a city gal, lived her whole life in a Bronx apartment. The concept of a dog hardly appealed to her, but the promise of a house in the suburbs certainly did. We had a deal. If I bought her a home in the suburbs, I could have a dog!

After a short time working in the family business (the phone company), I accepted a job with a pharmaceutical house in Philadelphia. The purchase of a house in Meadowbrook, Pennsylvania, soon followed. We bought a split level with three bedrooms on the twelve hundred block of George Road. It was a great house on a corner lot, with about a quarter acre of land. More than anything else we found a wonderful neighborhood. The welcome wagon came out as soon as we rolled in.

After settling in for a bit, I started my search for the big dog I always wanted. A coworker who raised Shetland Sheep Dogs had a litter. We went to check it out. Cassie, the pups' mother, was on site. When we walked in, Cassie went straight for Carole. She stood on her hind legs, planted her heavy paws on Carole's shoulders, and gave my wife a big kiss right on the lips. It makes for a funny memory, but that sank my chances of getting a Sheep Dog.

So I widened my search and decided to go with a St. Bernard. I loved the look and their history as Swiss rescue dogs. We got Murphy from a breeder when he was just a little thing. He had good coloring with the appropriate mix of white and brown. He had enough skin for his whole litter, but eventually he would grow into all that excess quite nicely. I couldn't wait to hang a barrel around his neck. He was one handsome dog.

I loved Murphy the moment I saw him, and it didn't take long for Carole to come on board too. He grew like a weed in all ways, shapes, and form. The dog I left when I went to work in the morning wasn't always the same dog I returned to at night. It was unbelievable how quickly he grew. He ate like a horse and made a mess like one too. Within a few weeks, he looked more like a pony than a dog. Eventually he would grow into those long legs and his body would fill out.

Carole loved him, especially for his soft coat. Like my twin brother Dick, Carole had suffered from polio as a child. She didn't have so bad a case as he did, and most people never knew, but the disease did its damage on her feet. After a long day on her feet at Holy Redeemer Hospital—where she worked as an operating room nurse—Carole would like nothing better than to rub her sore dogs on our dog's back.

When Carole wasn't soothing her feet on Murphy's fur, she was stroking his head, which he gladly planted in her lap. She would start on the top of his muzzle, moving her hand along the bridge of his nose, between his eyes, over his skull, and down to his shoulder blades. He would often fall asleep and always leave behind a pool of drool.

Murphy loved the attention of the neighborhood kids. Billy and Bobby Adshead, who lived across the street, and Jackie Reutemann, who lived next door, came over all the time. They would play in the yard and fuss over Murphy. They even brought Murphy a stuffed animal St. Bernard that was almost as big as he was.

As much as Carole and I got attention as the new people on the block, we were better known for our dog—sort of like how Kevin was later known for his golf ball–fetching German Shepherds. Yes, I was Murphy's dad.

As Murphy continued to grow, so did the collateral damage around the house. All dogs go through a destructive phase, but Murphy didn't just damage things, he destroyed them. One time, I took Carole shopping and left Murphy home alone with free rein in the family room. We returned a couple of hours later to a ransacked house. Bookcases were down, furniture was toppled over, and a dog obedience training book was half-eaten. I'm telling you, you couldn't have ransacked the house any better if you tried.

Murphy's mischief wasn't just limited to the house. I actually built him a home of his own inside his outside pen. It was a miniature Swiss chalet, complete with insulation and overhang. I had a Japanese maple planted next to it to provide ample shade. I thought it would be a great place for him to kick back and relax. He had other plans.

He ate the tree. I'm not kidding: he ate the tree. I came home one day and the foliage and branches were gone. That lovely tree looked like a twig. He did the same thing to his chalet, turning it into a shanty in a few short days.

Destruction aside, Murphy was a good soul. He only misbehaved when he was left alone. We figured he'd outgrow it as he matured. When my father would visit, Murphy would park himself by Dad's side. The two would while the time away. It was wonderful to see them together, and a chance for me to share with my father the gift he had given me years ago, a love of dogs.

I'm sure as my dad relaxed in the recliner and looked admiringly at Murphy, he felt good about his decision to raise us with dogs. His validation was seeing me, his son, repeating history. And I'm quite sure when he saw my infant son Christopher, staring at Murphy with wide, curious eyes, Dad knew another generation would make dogs an important part of their lives too.

Christopher was our first son. He was born in May of 1968. Murphy welcomed him into the fold with doggy kisses and a watchful eye. Wherever Christopher was, Murphy was always nearby. Murphy didn't have an overbearing suspicion of strangers coming near the baby like some other breeds do. He looked more like a huge, happy bouncer at a bar. Murphy loved his guardian role because he didn't really have to do anything other than be himself.

Baby Christopher on Murphy with Bob (left) and Albert Walsh

As Christopher started to crawl and pull himself up, naturally he saw Murphy as another mountain to climb. By now fully grown at two-hundred-plus pounds, Murphy could handle the load of another dozen pounds. The only thing we had to worry about was the tumble down, if Christopher lost his grip. But Murphy seemed to get the smooth ride part. He never moved fast or changed directions suddenly when the baby was on his back. He saved the roughhousing and rolling around for the bigger kids.

In the summer of 1969, we learned our family would be growing. Carole was pregnant with our second child, Kevin. Murphy must have known something was up because he started guarding Carole, much like he would Chris. It was further bonding for Carole and the dog. With Carole carrying more weight in the pregnancy, her tender feet hurt even more; so those foot rubs on Murphy's fur really were a joy at the end of the day. There was something else growing inside of another family member that would later have an impact on us all, and we never saw it coming.

A coworker and friend, Frank Krasovic, stopped by the house for a visit. After the usual chatting and snacking inside, we went outside to check up on Murphy, who was then eighteen months old. It was a warm, sunny day, and Murphy was doing what he did best—hang out. As we approached his chain-linked pen, Murphy got off his duff and ambled over to the gate. He was panting slightly and his pink tongue was moving in and out of his mouth in cadence with the pants. The usual drool dribbled off the sides of his jowls. His tail was wagging.

Standing next to Frank, I reached into Murphy's pen and gave him a pat on his furry brow. Murphy happily moved his head up and down, absorbing each touch. He put a little more wiggle in his wag and turned his attention to Frank, hopeful for much of the same.

Frank, a lover of dogs, looked on with a smile on his face and his hands at his side. When I was done with my greeting, Frank obliged Murphy's welcoming look. In a motion that I can only describe as unconscious and completely normal human behavior, Frank put his left hand on my shoulder and reached into the pen with his right to pet the dog.

In a frightening blur, Murphy attacked! Almost as soon as Frank reached, Murphy lunged, seizing Frank's hand and biting down with a ferocity I never knew my dog had in him. It all happened so horribly fast!

Frank screamed out in pain as Murphy sank his teeth in. And it wasn't just the bite. With Murphy's prodigious strength and weight, the biting and pulling motion pinned Frank's arm and body on top of the fence railing. I quickly reached over and grabbed Frank's wrist. As I frantically tried to pull my friend's hand out of the dog's mouth, Murphy turned his attention to me. No sooner did he let go of Frank's hand, Murphy had my hand in his mouth and was biting hard. In a mighty twist, I managed to pull my hand out before falling back from Murphy's pen.

I looked at my hand and saw a trickle of blood coming out of a puncture wound. I looked at Frank staring at his hand, which had more punctures and bleeding than mine. I saw Frank's face and he looked back at me. He was stunned, absolutely stunned, as if he couldn't believe what had just happened. Neither could I. Then I looked over at Murphy, peering back from the other side of the fence. He looked deranged, like a dog I never knew.

For a few moments, Frank and I said nothing. We were both taking big gulps of air, trying to settle down from the shock of it all. Blood droplets dotted our dress shirts, which were soaked in sweat. We were almost afraid to look at Murphy because of the horror of what just happened. But, fearing he might somehow try to get out of his pen and attack again, I think we felt compelled to keep an eye on him. Murphy didn't move, and before we knew it, we were inside the house cleaning ourselves up.

"Oh God, Frank, I'm so sorry," I told him as we scrubbed our wounds with soap at the kitchen sink. "I don't know what happened."

Frank was hurting but sympathetic. "I know, I know," he said anxiously as he toweled off, "it's just like all of a sudden he flipped a switch."

And that's exactly what happened. There were no warning signs that we could see. Murphy simply snapped. The whole episode took maybe ten seconds, but it seemed to last forever. I walked Frank to his car and said goodbye. He never held it against me. I think he knew how sorry and troubled I was by what happened.

After Frank left, I sat for a few moments pondering what happened and what I would have to do next. The good news was we weren't seriously hurt. Had we been on the inside of the kennel, who knows? Murphy was big enough to overpower just about anybody, including me—his master. It was a scary thought compounded by the reality that we had a baby and another one on the way. I remain thankful that the dog had not attacked a child. When I think about it, it gives me the shivers.

Seeking solutions, I contacted a local kennel that specialized in boarding St. Bernards. It suggested a two-week isolation period. Retrieving Murphy from his pen was not done without fear and trepidation of his turning on me once again. Without incident, I got him out and into the car. It was a nerve-wracking ride considering what had previously happened, and that Murphy was in really close quarters with me. I kept one eye on him in the rearview mirror and the other one on the road.

During the incarceration, one of the dog handlers said that Murphy was by far the most vicious animal he had ever encountered. Our dog even tried to attack other female St. Bernards in adjoining runs. But why? Why? Why? It was quickly determined that after the two-week period, Murphy would have to be put down. I requested an autopsy. The finding showed that he was in severe pain due to a breeding fault. His brain had grown larger than his skull could accommodate.

Subsequently, I became aware that a veterinarian at a prominent Pennsylvania clinic had seen this fault in other poorly bred animals. I told a coworker the story of Murphy's sudden change in disposition at eighteen months of age. Shortly thereafter, a neighbor's St. Bernard—who was also eighteen months old—attacked his daughter. I felt terrible for him and his girl. At the same time, I was greatly relieved we put Murphy to sleep before he inflicted more damage than he had already.

SIX

Susie (Dog on Loan), Daisy, and Danielle

KEVIN

In the early and mid-1970s, the years that we were without a dog, our next-door neighbors were so kind to us. Vince, Evie, Peggy, and Jackie Reutemann were dog people too. They offered us unlimited visits from Susie, their copper-colored Lab mix. Susie wasn't overly playful, but she loved to be around people. Her presence was her present. Susie loved to be hugged, and she was quick with kisses that weren't as messy as Murphy's, before Murphy lost his mind.

A narrow strip of grass separated our driveway from the Reutemanns. Quite often, we'd be out playing ball on the driveway and Susie would just wander over. We even had a food and water bowl for her. She'd come into the house and hang out for hours. When it was time for her to go home, we'd just open the back door and say, "Susie, go home."

Susie would walk out the door, around the brick wall that semi-enclosed our patio, across our driveway, and

Susie, the neighbor's dog with Bob, Chris, and Kevin, 1975

around the pine trees that separated our properties. When she reached her patio, she'd bark. Vince or Evie would open the door and let her inside.

I was four or five years old and Susie was the first dog I had a relationship with. "Love Susie like she's your dog," my dad would tell me.

"I do, but when can we have our own dog?" I'd ask in return.

"We will, when the time is right," he'd responded.

That's about the same as a "we'll see" answer. Both are non-definite. There's no good reason to hope for what you want anytime soon. Our pet experience after Murphy was Susie on loan and window shopping at the pet store. We all longed for something more.

After Sunday Mass at St. Hilary's in Rydal, we'd often drive to Oxford Valley Mall in Langhorne, Pennsylvania, to have lunch at Farrell's. After dessert, we'd take a walk over to the pet store, imagining what life would be like if we could have a dog of our own again.

My brother Chris inflicted the bulk of the emotional pressure on our parents. "I remember crying in my room at night saying that I missed Murphy. I looked through old photo albums, but that didn't cut it. We also had a big red *Encyclopedia of Dogs* and I'd study the different breeds," Chris says.

BOB

Oh I definitely felt the pressure. I wanted another dog too, but we were concerned that Christopher might have allergies. We told him we'd have to wait until he was twelve years old, and then we would try again. But that seemed like an eternity.

We were also pretty sure that if we got another dog, it would have to be a small breed that didn't shed. We had another neighbor who had a Cairn Terrier with a wonderful disposition and minimal shedding. I did some research and was pleased with what I found. Of course I remembered Toto, a cute Cairn that followed Dorothy around in *The Wizard of Oz*.

So I talked it over with Carole and we decided it was time. It was 1976 and Chris's eighth birthday was coming up. It was the perfect opportunity for a new addition to the family and a chance to give the boys a job around the house.

Carole found a beautiful Cairn in the mall pet store. We reserved the dog and then set about concocting a ruse that would make for a wonderful birthday surprise for Chris. On Chris's birthday in May, we went to Farrell's for dinner with some of the neighborhood kids. During the course of the meal, I excused myself and went to the pet store. I paid for the dog and gave the store attendant a beautiful red bow and sign to put on the Cairn that we would name Daisy.

We knew for sure that as soon as the party was over, Chris would ask if we could stop by the pet store to check out the puppies. Off we went for a quick run-through. Chris ran into the store and checked the larger animals first. Then he stopped dead in his tracks in front of a cage where a little ball of fur was happily grinning, knowing that her life was about to change for the better.

The bow was chewed in half, but still hanging around the pup's neck. So was the sign that read, "Happy Birthday Chris." It was a sterling moment for both Carole and me. The look on his face spoke of confusion since he knew he was only eight, and not yet twelve. I asked him if he knew what the sign meant. The boy was greatly confused. It was too good to be true. But it was truly true. It was Christopher's pup.

Chris Walsh is Bob's son and Kevin's older brother.
His current dogs are Rio and another Daisy.

"I was shocked and felt disbelief when I saw a dog with my name on her cage!" Chris remembers. "Supposedly, I was allergic to dogs and couldn't have one until I was twelve. How did they know the allergy was going to go away at age twelve?"

BOB

We named the dog Daisy. Daisy was like a breath of fresh air. She came home with us inside of Carole's purse. She made our house a home once again. Daisy housetrained easily, was very obedient, and loved to play. She had all the great characteristics. I remember one time when she disappeared. We searched all of her haunts, but still no Daisy. I could hear a whimper in the kitchen, but I couldn't see her. In the closet I looked, no Daisy. Eventually, I found her wagging her tail inside the cabinet below the kitchen sink. Love and kisses were the tale of the day.

CHRIS

My fondest memory of Daisy was that she was my dog. There's just something about the concept of mine. She loved to play ball too. Though not a Retriever by breed, she could catch up to the ball as well as any other dog. She couldn't catch it in her mouth because her mouth was too small for that—rarely would she bring the ball back. Instead, it was more like a chase it and kill it game. That giant red *Encyclopedia of Dogs* that we had on the family room shelf told me all I needed to know about a Cairn's characteristics. I learned that Cairn Terriers were bred to hunt small animals in burrows. I thought that was cool. My dog was a hunter!

KEVIN

We often took Daisy to Pennock Woods, now the place of a posh housing development with large wooded lots. But back in the seventies it was just "The Woods." It was the only place where we could let Daisy off leash. We'd ride our bicycles on the trails and she would chase us. We'd turn rocks over in streams to gather crayfish. Daisy would move in for a closer look and sniff. That ended one day when a larger crustacean's pincher got either side of Daisy's nostril. Her days of hunting crayfish waned, but certainly not her love of getting wet. Daisy would splash around and then shimmy shake the wetness off on us.

Most of our fun in The Woods happened in an open space that we called The Army Field. Years prior, the Army National Guard practiced there with its tanks, hence the name. The Army Field was home to deer, fox, ticks, a variety of vermin, and lots of dirt mounds from which we jumped our bikes while pretending to be Evel Knievel.

Daisy stayed with us much of the time, but more often than not she followed her nose wherever it took her. One time it took her down what appeared to be a fox hole How she fit I still don't know. Chris and I, with friends Peter Van Buren and Steve Phillips, just looked at each other dumbfounded.

"Where did she go?" Chris asked Peter.

"I dunno," he shrugged.

"I think it probably opens up underground," Steve offered.

"Opens up to what?" Chris wanted to know.

"Maybe a fox's den," Steve theorized.

Whatever it was, I was thinking it wasn't going to end well. If there was a fox underground, wouldn't it attack and kill Daisy when she reached its den? How then would we retrieve her body? Chris looked like he was going to cry, as if he too knew it was a cat-out-of-the-bag situation working in reverse.

We thought about what to do. Should we go home and tell a parent? Or get a shovel and start digging? We were so scared that more than anything we just froze and exchanged confused looks. After about ten minutes of doing nothing, Daisy saved us by rumbling up from underground. Her nose was pancaked with dirt, and she was panting heavily. She looked happy and hardly the worse for wear. What happened underground we'll never know, but I know this much, we never let her run down a fox hole again.

BOB

Daisy was such a great addition to the clan. She walked, she ran, she played, she loved, and she didn't shed. The kids loved her to death, as did I. Even Carole quickly grew to love her. One characteristic that I didn't like was that she liked to run away. "Daisy, Daisy. Come here pup!" I'd often call.

One time she ran across the very busy Washington Lane in Meadowbrook where cars go fast. She narrowly missed being hit more than once. We knew we had to keep her away from Washington Lane. And then one day her luck ran out.

CHRIS

I'll never forget the day Daisy died. We were all out playing on the driveway. Mom had been fussing over Daisy that afternoon. Boy did she love the attention, rolling over for Mom to scratch her little pink belly. But Mom was on her way out to run an errand. We were caught up in our games. It was only when one of us caught a fleeting glimpse of fur dart by that we realized Daisy had gotten out of the house. She was chasing after Mom as she pulled away in the car. We all screamed for Daisy, but she was locked in and focused on her prey—the car! Dropping our bikes and balls, we all gave chase, knowing that Mom was headed toward treacherous Washington Lane.

Another car came up behind Mom's. Daisy then locked in on that one. Time seemed to freeze as we ran across the lawn and the Reutemanns' driveway. But it was too late. As we chased and screamed for Daisy and the cars to stop, Daisy was caught by the rear tire of the trailing car.

We approached cautiously, scared of what we might find. Was there a chance that she was okay? Fear of what we might see was quickly dispensed by our desire to help and save the dog we loved. As we approached, we saw the blood coming from Daisy's ear and she began to convulse. Mom heard our screams and got out of her car. She could see the fear in our eyes and she looked equally stunned.

We acted quickly. We wrapped Daisy in a towel and put her inside the car on the backseat. Mom and I exchanged desperate glances. I think right then we realized she wouldn't be coming home that night. The trip to the vet seemed like an eternity. We said our prayers, probably more on that ride than the whole prior year. We'd said them in hopes of a miracle. But it wasn't to be.

Daisy's last gift to us was a lesson in coping with loss. We were young. It hurt. It left a pit in our stomachs. But it was that loss, the emptiness that we all felt that made us realize the need and place for dogs in our family.

BOB

We all wanted Daisy back. But finding a dog just like her, or something close, was really tough. She was one of a kind. I definitely preferred Cairns with gray-colored coats, but one characteristic of the breed is their coats change color. What you start with isn't what you finish with.

In the late seventies, I traveled extensively, primarily to the United Kingdom. My search pattern broadened, yet I still couldn't find a gray Cairn Terrier. A British friend offered to check on the Queen's breeder of Cairns, but it didn't have a gray female. What the heck, I'd take a purple Cairn if it came with a royal lineage. But it just wasn't meant to be in Britain either.

In 1980, I heard about Betty Hyslop, the Canadian Grand Dame of Cairn Terriers. I called Betty and told her what I was looking for. She indicated that since I wanted "just" a house pet, she would not consider selling one of her Cairns to me. She did, however, suggest that I contact Edith Skellet, a breeder and close friend who lived in Ontario, Canada.

I called Edith Skellet and she said she had a two-year-old gray female named Molly who was available. It was late December, and I had time off from work for the holidays. The kids were off from school. I asked if we could come up to see her dog. "Sure," she said.

I went out to the Abington Pharmacy and bought some roadmaps. I started plotting the course to Canada and was delighted to discover that Niagara Falls was not far from the route we would take. With a stop at the falls, I figured it would be eight to nine hours before we arrived at Cairnmoor Kennel. We'd travel the next day, but, of course, the excitement of the pending trip kept Chris and Kevin up through the night.

The next morning, we woke up around 7:30. Carole rose with us and made me eggs and toast. Chris poured himself a bowl of Cocoa Krispies. Kevin opted for Cap'n Crunch. As I sipped on my second cup of Taster's Choice instant coffee, I could see the national weather map on the screen of our small black-and-white kitchen TV. Willard Scott was pointing at a weather system in the upper Midwest that was making its way east and looked to be arriving in the next eighteen to twenty-four hours.

"Come on boys, finish up," I ordered.

"Why? What's the hurry?" Kevin wanted to know.

"There's a storm that's coming our way, and we don't want to get caught in it. We don't have much time to get up there and come home. You do want to get your new dog today don't you?" I asked, imploringly.

"Oh yes!" the boys said, shoveling the cereal into their mouths twice as fast.

After cleaning up after breakfast, brushing teeth, and taking necessary bathroom breaks, we loaded up my brown 1977 Chevrolet Supreme. We stopped for gas at Hale's Gulf 76 on the corner of Welsh Road and Huntingdon Pike in Bethayres. Chuck Hale came out to pump the regular unleaded. Donny Hale looked up from under a car's hood in the garage and waved like he always does.

"Going somewhere?" Chuck asked, noticing the blankets in the backseat of the car.

"Yes, we're going to Canada," I told him.

"Is that right? What for?"

"Well, we're getting another dog and we have to go to the breeder to pick it up."

"That's a long way to go for a dog. It must be a very special dog," he said while handing over the carbon receipt.

"It is," I told him smiling and looking in the rearview mirror to see the boys doing the same.

Not long after pulling out of the gas station, we hopped onto the Pennsylvania Turnpike. I could bore you with the driving details, but for brevity sake, let's just say we played name games and talked about sports before turning northwest through the Pocono Mountains of Pennsylvania and on through central and western New York.

We arrived at Niagara Falls at the most perfect time. It was late afternoon, and the gas lamps that ringed the viewing points from the opposite side of the falls were just starting to glow as the sky was dark from overcast. What's more, a mist from the pounding falls was drifting over to the viewing area, freezing on the walkways, railings, and lampposts. It truly was a winter wonderland.

Naturally the kids treated the viewing deck as an ice skating rink. My boys were not alone. One particularly reckless kid who—based on his accent—had to have been from Brooklyn, knocked an older gent on his tail. It would have been very unfortunate had the elderly man been injured and not laughing about it. I think everyone appreciated the spectacle of one of nature's greatest wonders. I know I did. And it wouldn't be long before we experienced another wonder, albeit a smaller one, on our own.

KEVIN

When we stopped at the border, I remember one of the officers having a particularly difficult time believing that we'd come all the way from Pennsylvania and were about to enter Canada to pick up a dog.

"You're picking up a dog, eh?" he asked with a hint of doubt in his tone.

"That's right," Dad told the man with a badge.

"And it's your dog?" the officer wanted to know.

"No, not yet," Dad explained. "It will be when we pick it up."

"So, your dog is not lost, eh?"

"No, our dog is not lost," my dad said exasperatedly. "We don't have a dog right now. We're going to buy one from a breeder. That will be our dog."

"Do you have paperwork to that effect? Your purpose of being here," he pressed.

"No I don't. I just know that we're going to Cairnmoor Kennel and they're expecting us shortly," Dad said, clearly becoming upset with the questioning.

"Okay. Go on through safely," he said while waving us through the checkpoint.

"Are we not allowed to be in this country?" I asked my dad.

"No. No. No, it's not that. We're allowed to be in the country. It's just they want to make sure everyone has a specific purpose for coming across the border," Dad said, feeling only slightly less annoyed with me than with the border officer.

Now safely away from the border, we had another issue to deal with—the metric system. The speed limit was listed in kilometers, instead of miles per hour. "Do you boys know how to convert kilometers per hour to miles per hour?" Dad wanted to know.

Neither of us did. So Dad figured he'd just go whatever number he saw on the speed limit signs in miles per hour. Most read 60 km/h. It didn't take long to figure out we were moving quite fast through a small city. I'm pretty sure Dad didn't mind, because the questioning at the border set us back a bit in time. Chris and I were thrilled to see our dad driving so fast because we had never really seen it before. Dad was one of the slowest drivers we knew. He drove the speed limit just about all the time. On top of that, he didn't allow us to play the radio.

As we were zipping along at about 60 miles per hour, heads were turning from pedestrians walking along sidewalks. The same was true of the motorists in the cars we were leaving in our dust. Within a few minutes, I noticed a white car pulling out of a side street and catching up fast. Then I saw flashing blue lights. The local police had us pegged for speeding.

"Sir, do you realize how fast you were traveling?" the approaching police officer asked in a much friendlier tone than the border services officer.

"No, I really don't," Dad confessed. "In fact I'm not sure I can figure out your signs and the speed limit."

"Well you were going excessively fast. Don't you have kilometers per hour on your speedometer?"

"No, I don't think so," Dad answered.

"Okay then. I'm going to write you a ticket for going 88 instead of the 90 that I clocked you at. Just try to keep your speed around 30 miles per hour and you'll be okay."

With that the officer handed us a ticket, and off we went with him in tow for a couple of blocks. Not a moment after the police officer peeled off, Chris announced, "Hey see those blue numbers below the bigger white numbers on the speedometer? What are they?"

It was then my dad had a little fit. "Jiminy Christmas," he said slapping the wheel and shaking his head, "we had a speedometer for kilometers all along!"

I started to laugh and pretty soon we all were. It had been an eventful day and soon we'd be arriving at the kennel.

We pulled up to Cairnmoor Kennel, which doubled as a small house at the end of a gravel driveway. Mr. Skellet answered the door holding a small dark gray Cairn Terrier in his left hand. As I stood on the steps outside the door I wondered if that was our dog. So I asked, "Is that Molly?"

"No, no. This is Higgs, a boy," Mr. Skellet laughed heartily.

"Hicks?" I asked, not sure whether I heard correctly.

"No. Higgs, short for Higgins," he said.

"Oh that's cool. That's kind of a different name. Is he one of the dogs for sale?"

"Oh no, no, no," Mr. Skellet said proudly. "He's my boy. He's the one dog I get to keep. I gotta have a boy."

BOB

Edith Skellet welcomed us into her home. It was nicely kept, warmly lit, and traditional in color and décor. Mrs. Skellet was a wonderful hostess. She brought me coffee and hot chocolate for Chris and Kevin. We'd come to see Molly and had all but counted on taking her home that night. But there was a problem. Molly wasn't the color match I was looking for. Perhaps it had something to do with Molly going into heat and a Cairn's tendency to change color in their coat.

I was very disheartened. Mrs. Skellet asked if I'd consider a reddish tan two-year-old female. What the heck, I thought. We'd already come this far in time, distance, and emotion not to try. The boys seemed very upset. None of us wanted to go home empty handed. Mrs. Skellet excused herself. The boys sat quietly, stirring their hot chocolate. I was stirring inside.

A minute later, Mrs. Skellet returned with Danielle, a mature, nicely trained animal. I liked her. So did the boys. She took affection well but wasn't overly generous in giving it. I liked that because it showed restraint, something you don't find all that often in younger dogs.

"Boys, could you be happy with Danielle?" I asked. "I know she's not as playful as Molly, but she's a very good dog and I think she'd fit right in with us. Plus, I think Mom would much prefer a calm dog."

The boys were sold and so was I. As I pulled out my checkbook to pay for our new dog, Mrs. Skellet offered to put us up for the night as a lake-effect snow storm was in the forecast. It was a very nice offer, but I declined. I figured we could beat the storm and ride on adrenaline the rest of the way back to Pennsylvania.

Mr. and Mrs. Skellet stood on the steps of their home and waved goodbye, as we piled back into the car. The boys fussed over who would hold the dog. Danielle didn't seem to care which boy held her, or if neither one did. That was the type of dog she was, no frills—not then, not ever.

I knew we made the right choice in Danielle and had faith Carole would accept, and maybe learn to love her, too. The boys may dispute it, but there's no doubt in my mind that Dannie, as we mostly called her, was my dog. She was unobtrusive and like an old shoe, always comfortable and nearby. She fit right in with the family. Life was beautiful and in balance, once again.

Because she was so little and hardly shed at all, Dannie pretty much could go and relax wherever she wished. Her favorite spot was a forest green reading chair in our formal living room. The fact that she wanted to sleep on the chair wasn't so much the problem—it's what she did to the seat cushion to make it more to her liking.

One day Carole walked into the living room, horrified to find the remnants of Dannie's work. "Oh my God! That little dog dug a hole in my chair!" Carole screamed in agony.

I came running and saw the space Dannie carved out of the cushion. She dug a hole in the center of the cushion so she could settle in more snugly. Carole was having a fit, which I understood. But the fix was relatively simple. When special guests came over, we just reversed the cushion and no one ever knew.

As laid back as Danielle was, from time to time, she revealed a toughness and guardianship about her. One day Kevin came home all excited that he had a job. He was commissioned by a kindly neighbor to look after their pet parakeet. We said, sure! He picked up the bird and proudly brought it home. We had forgotten about Dannie, who proceeded to give the bird the evil eye as it sat on its perch inside the cage on the kitchen counter.

She barked at the bird and seemed to be plotting an attack. Realizing that this was no way for the bird to enjoy its visit, or for us to live in such tension, I decided to take the bird downstairs and park the cage in my workshop. Out of sight, out of mind, right? Not exactly.

The parakeet chirped constantly, and its sound could be heard through the floor. Danielle expertly located the spot directly over the bird's cage. In no time flat she'd dug a hole in the carpet right where our formal living room and dining room connected with an open entryway. She was working on the floorboard when I stopped her. Through a crack in the floorboard you could see and hear the parakeet singing up a storm. Kevin got his $10 for bird sitting, and I got stuck with a $250 carpet repair. But we learned.

Danielle preferred to be inside the house, but when she went outside to do her business, she made it her business to check out her turf. One time, Kevin came into the house looking as if he'd seen a ghastly attack. He did, or at least the aftermath of one. Danielle had intercepted a squirrel on its way to our trash cans parked right outside our garage doors. She didn't just kill the animal—she ripped its chest open. I'm just glad Carole didn't see it. Danielle had parked the carcass right by Carole's driver's-side car door as if it were a prized trophy.

Hoping to avoid future cleanups like that, I placed a small bell on Danielle's collar. It was my way to alert her prey that she was coming and you better get out of Dodge fast. It worked for most critters, but not for one scary opossum.

We were returning from a visit with the Adshead family across the street. Dannie and an opossum spied each other and had a showdown. Neither was willing to back off. The hair stood up straight along the spines of each animal. Dannie barked, the opossum hissed. Thinking it might not end well, I grabbed Dannie by the scruff of her neck and she relaxed. I'm sure she saw herself as the consummate victor. I was proud.

KEVIN

Dannie had some quirks. She particularly liked to lick my feet. I often had sweaty feet thanks to thirty-six holes of caddying and my own rounds of golf. I think it was the salt that she was after, but who knows for sure. All I know is that whenever I'd take off my white sweat socks, Dannie would come on over and give my dogs a bath.

"That is so gross!" my brother Chris would say in protest.

"Why?" I'd ask naively. "It's probably good for her in some way, kind of like when dogs eat grass to settle their stomachs."

"No, no way! Cut it out, that's disgusting and the lapping sound is annoying too," Chris argued.

My brother's unease only encouraged me to seek Danielle out, if she didn't find me first. This is what brothers do—find ways to annoy each other. I found the foot wash relaxing. It kind of tickled, and it got the funk

Michael Walsh with Danielle, 1980

off my feet. Dannie did it for years. Chris is still annoyed by it. Awesome!

We got a lot of good years of love and service out of Danielle. She guarded the crib of my younger brother Michael, who was born in 1977. She did the same with the front and back doors of our house. Nobody could set foot on our property without Dannie sending off the barking alarm. I'm not sure she could have stopped an intruder from coming inside, but I have no doubt she would have died trying.

It was 1987, and I had my driver's license for a little more than a year. Danielle really enjoyed taking rides in my Dodge 600 convertible. I noticed Dannie had been coughing consistently for a week or more, and I thought it would be good to go for a ride to get her some fresh air. When I asked, "Do you want to go for a ride, Dannie?" she walked right over to the door.

It was a Saturday afternoon in the fall of my senior year of high school. I drove Dannie over to Abington High School's football field after a varsity game. She needed to get out of the house; I needed to catch up with friends to see what the plans were for that night. Usually, when we took drives, Dannie would stand on her hind legs in the backseat, resting her front paws on the arm rest. She would extend her head and neck above the sides of the car, catching the full breeze in her face with the convertible top down. But on this day she stayed below the wake of the air rushing by.

I pulled into the side parking lot and maneuvered into a space. Grabbing the leash, I jumped out and made my way over to the passenger side. Dannie was really coughing now. Did all that swirling wind somehow send a hairball down her throat? Reaching into the backseat I lifted her out. Hoping to move along whatever might be stuck, I gently stroked Danielle's throat. I felt two lumps on either side.

A few of my friends came over to say hello, including Jamie Wagner. He played center on the football team and still had smudges of eye black on his cheeks. Sandra Saylor, a cheerleader, came over to say hello and to pet Dannie. Dannie accepted pats on the head, but they only seemed to exacerbate her cough.

"Oh poor dog," Sandra said. "I hope you feel better."

We didn't stay long at the field and certainly not long enough to find out where the get-togethers were that night. I wanted to get Dannie to the vet. Her coughing had gone on long enough, and those lumps in her throat made me think she needed some strong medicine to make her feel better.

"Come on, Danielle. Let's take you to the doctor so you can start feeling better," I said to her as I loaded her back into the car.

When we got home, I asked my mom where the emergency phone numbers were. Mom pulled out a three-by-five index card with the numbers of every imaginable emergency service written in red ink, in Mom's exquisite cursive writing. The card was a leftover from the days when we required babysitters. Mom would tuck the emergency numbers card behind the rotary phone mounted on the kitchen wall. The only number I could ever remember calling was Hopewell Veterinary Hospital in Jenkintown. It was about halfway down the list.

As I dialed away, Dannie made her way over to her water bowl with faux wood paneling on the side. She took a couple of laps from the top of the water and quickly started coughing again. It was clear the water did nothing to soothe her sore throat. It probably only made it worse. The attack didn't last long because she got stuck in the middle of a cough. She stretched her mouth by opening it wide and closing it a couple of times. Something else overrode the action. Dannie's stomach convulsed and her body tensed. What looked like a mighty effort produced a small trickle of yellow bile.

Dannie looked tired and embarrassed. Before I could grab some paper towels to clean up her mess, she had already started cleaning by licking at the little puddle.

"It's okay, Dannie. I got it," I told her as I stroked her head with one hand and wiped up the mess with the other. Her eyes looked so sad.

I picked up the phone and dialed Hopewell's number. Hoping we might be lucky to get a Monday appointment, we did better. The girl on the line at the veterinary hospital asked me to describe Danielle's symptoms. When I did, she said, "Come over right away."

As I was walking with Dannie to the back door, my dad intercepted me. "Where are you going?" he asked.

"To the vet," I told him. "I want to get Dannie checked out because of her cough. I also felt some lumps on her neck."

"Let me go with you," Dad said.

My dad bent down and stroked Dannie's head while feeling the lumps in her throat with his other hand. Dannie looked up at Dad with fear in her eyes and hope in her heart that he could somehow make her feel better. A little tremor worked its way through Dannie's body. It couldn't have been from the temperature because it was warm that day. Dad scooped the dog up and walked to my car. He climbed inside the passenger's side with Danielle in his arms.

We drove in silence for much of the way. About halfway to the animal hospital, my dad asked, "Have you noticed she hasn't been eating as much lately?"

"Yes. She's leaving food in her bowl, and it does look like she's lost weight," I told him.

"What about her hair? Does it look like she's lost some hair too?" he asked.

"Yeah I guess so. Look at the back of her body. It looks patchy."

Five minutes later we pulled into the parking lot of Hopewell Veterinary Hospital on Cedar Road. Dad carried Dannie on his right arm, holding her in the palm of his hand and on the underside of his forearm, much like a bowler handles a heavy ball.

"Hi. I'm the one who just called about the dog with a bad cough," I told the girl at the front desk.

"Oh yes. Come with me," she said leading us to an examining room.

We sat on hard, easy-to-clean plastic chairs that no dog could destroy. Dannie sat on Dad's lap. He ran his hand from her brow, down her back and back and forth. She shot a quick look my way and looked every bit as concerned as she had a few minutes before while at home. Dad and I said nothing.

After five minutes of waiting, the silence was broken by the door opening. A young doctor walked in. She couldn't have been much more than thirty years old, if that. She extended her hand with a warm greeting and a caring look at Danielle.

"How long has it been since she started losing her hair and weight?" she wanted to know.

"Uh, probably about two weeks," I answered.

"And her cough has gotten progressively worse at the same time?"

"Yes it has."

The doctor gently reached under Dannie's snout and caressed her neck while sliding her hand down toward the dog's breast. "How long has she had these lumps in her throat? Do you know?"

"I don't know how long she's had them. I just found them today. But I imagine they've probably been around a while, considering how big they are. I guess I just haven't touched her there in a while," I explained.

The vet felt around her other glands and found evidence of tumors in each place. Finally she said, "I am sorry but I have really bad news. I suspect your dog has lymphatic sarcoma. I can't be 100 percent sure without a biopsy, but she has lumps in her throat and in all of her lymph nodes. When you have lumps in all the lymph nodes, 95 percent of the time it's cancerous."

I felt like all the air was sucked out of my lungs. I thought we were coming to the vet to get some medicine, and all would be well. I did not plan for this. We were not done.

"What are our options?" my dad asked.

"We'd have to biopsy to prove it is cancer, which I'm almost sure it is. That would be followed by chemotherapy. The chemotherapy is expensive and there's no guarantee it'll work. In fact, with many of the older dogs, it just accelerates their death, based on their existing condition," she answered.

"How far along do you think she is based on what you've seen and felt?" Dad asked.

"Pretty far."

"If not chemotherapy, what would be your recommendation then?"

"I would manage the condition and treat the pain with meds for as long as she's comfortable. But if she's not comfortable, or when she becomes uncomfortable, my recommendation would be euthanasia."

My dad looked at me with his steely blue eyes and asked, "Kevin, do you think Dannie has been suffering lately?"

"Yes," I answered, as a chill shot down my spine.

Danielle I'm sure could sense the gravity of the situation from the tone of our voices and the many hands in many places on her body. She looked at me, widened her brown eyes and spoke to me in expression alone. She looked worried sick. She was sick and I'm sure her heart hurt as much as mine.

"If we decide to put her down, how do we go about doing it?" Dad asked. "Do you do it now? Or do we make an appointment?"

"I have a technician here with me so we could do it now," the doctor said, "or if you'd like to take her home for a little while and think about everything, you could make an appointment for later."

"Would you excuse us for about five minutes?" my dad asked.

"Oh sure, take your time. When you want me to come back, just knock on the door; it's pretty quiet now, so I'll hear it and come back down the hall to you."

When the doctor left, my dad placed both of his hands around Danielle's head, cupping it like a chalice. He gave her a few rubs with his thumbs and fingers and lifted her head while lowering his face to hers. He looked right into her eyes and stared for a few moments. Neither he nor she blinked. It was so touching, so loving and so heartbreaking.

"You're a good girl, Danielle," he said while undoing her collar.

That's when I knew Danielle wasn't coming home with us. As my dad pulled her collar away, familiar sounds flooded the tense air. The jingle jangle of her chain and the tinkling of the warning bell tolled for the last time. I didn't really know what to say because I had never had to say goodbye to a living creature before their time.

"Just tell her what a good dog she's been," my dad said, seeing that I was having trouble putting something together.

"Oh, Dannie. You're such a good girl," I said as I leaned in to her face while stroking the back of her small head behind her ears. "You've been such a good dog for us. I love you."

What I couldn't say in words, I did in touch. Dannie just looked at me with such a worried face and a twitching nose, as if she knew what was coming. Dad knocked on the door and the doctor came in. She saw the collar in his hands and didn't have to ask what our decision was. Dad walked out the door and I followed. I felt Dannie's eyes the whole way out.

When we reached the parking lot, the sun was setting on the day and a life. We got to the car and I opened my dad's door. He lowered himself into the passenger seat, and I closed the door behind him. When I swung around to the driver's side, a light coming from a single window at the veterinary hospital caught my eye. Danielle was looking through the glass at me.

There were two women inside the room with Dannie, the doctor and the technician. Neither saw me on the outside looking in. The technician approached the window and pulled down a thin shade. Three shadowy figures were visible through the shade as dusk fell. Two were tall, one was short. It was obvious who was who, and what was happening. Seconds later the shortest shadow disappeared. My dog was gone. Age and illness took her from us.

Dad and I rode home in mostly silence. By now we were good at that. After a couple of minutes, I had to say something because the quiet was killing me.

"Did that hurt you as much as it hurt me?" I asked my dad.

"Oh yes. That was really tough, but you know what? We did the right thing. No dog should have to suffer. She was too good a dog."

Dad was right about that one; and he was right to sense that what I thought would be a simple trip to the vet for medicine might not be so simple after all. I'm not sure I could have handled that ending alone. In the end I didn't have to. Just like my dad didn't have to dispose of Claudia when he found her dead in a hole in his backyard decades earlier, his father showed up just in time, providing wisdom and strength, and a profound opportunity for father and son to connect on the most personal of levels.

SEVEN

Susie: The Gold Standard

BOB

"That's it, no more dogs," my wife, Carole, announced when Kevin and I returned from putting down Danielle at the vet.

"What?" we asked collectively.

"I don't want any more dogs. With Kevin going away to college at Purdue University next year, there won't be anyone left to take care of another dog," Mom said.

"Wait a minute," I reminded her, "Michael is ten. I was taking care of dogs when I was six. Kevin and Christopher did the same right around the same age. Michael is capable and more than willing to raise another dog."

Kevin and Michael were witnesses and lobbied too. But Carole would have none of it. "Those are my wishes and I don't want anyone to disobey my wishes. I've put up with dogs long enough. Don't test me on this one," she said firmly.

For different reasons, it was disheartening to hear. First and foremost, it made us all wonder if a big part of our life and culture was over. With a few gaps in time, dogs had always been a part of my life, and certainly the lives of our children. They weren't just animals; they were an extension of our family. They guarded our house, slept in and under our beds and cribs, connected us with neighbors in ways that humans couldn't. We couldn't always count on the moods and the reliability of the people around us, but we could always count on our dogs. They were a constant. Now, in an instant, it all seemed to be gone.

"Mom, don't be silly," Kevin said in good humor. "Look at it this way. With a dog, at least someone is always happy to see you when you come home."

That produced a smirk in Carole because it reminded her that we can all be pills to one another at times. However, she quickly tried to turn that smirk into a furrowed brow and said, "Nope. We're done with dogs."

So maybe Carole was done with dogs, but clearly the kids and I weren't. "What do you think of that?" I asked Kevin away from Carole.

"She'll come around," Kevin said, "she's just reacting emotionally and is probably fearful of a new dog and the usual puppy damage and messes."

That I could understand. Older dogs spoil us. They trick us into feeling that they're really not a lot of work. Aside from a belly rub, a bowl of bland food and the occasional walk around the block, they don't need much from us. For that little investment, they reward us a hundred-fold. Of course we all forget the growing pains that got them there—chewed shoes, soiled carpets, home escapes, and lengthy searches.

The Walsh family (left to right) Kevin, Chris, Bob, Carole, and Michael Walsh, 1989

Before a dog starts its sunset into geriatric age and failing health, our best time with them is similar to the years we enjoyed with our kids after diaper duty ended and preadolescence began. Parents have to go through a lot to get to the good stuff. Eventually we have our fill of that as our bodies and our patience say enough's enough. Apparently Carole had had enough, but we (the children and I) were ready for more.

KEVIN

It was a couple of months after Danielle died, the spring of 1988, and I remember my dad telling me, "Hey I've been looking at Golden Retrievers lately. There's a breeder up in Quakertown that has a litter. Want to take a ride up and take a look?" he asked.

"Yeah!" I said. "What about Mom, though?"

"We'll worry about that later. Let's just go have a look," Dad said.

So, with that, we climbed into Dad's canary yellow Chrysler LeBaron convertible and took the forty-minute ride north up Route 309. Michael came along as he was just as interested. If we pulled the trigger, Michael would eventually be the primary caretaker of the dog.

I had overheard my dad chatting with his good friend Lesher Valentine, who grew up with Golden Retrievers and whelped a couple of litters over the years. Mr.

Valentine loved Goldens. His dogs were always well-behaved and as sweet as could be. My dad really valued the advice of Mr. Valentine, so I wasn't surprised Dad was becoming increasingly interested in getting back in on the dog game, with an upgrade in size from Cairn Terriers.

We drove up the gravel driveway of the breeder to the welcoming chorus of puppies chirping. The breeder was a nice woman with young children of her own. Her son must have been three or four years old. He loved the puppies and they loved him.

"Puppies! Puppies! Puppies!" he said over and over as the puppies climbed all over him with whipping tails and smothering kisses.

Michael and I joined the fun. Simply crouching down started an ambush of sandy-colored dogs with eyes like marbles and charcoal chipped noses. The males muscled their way to the front, but every dog made sure to get in a greeting.

"How much do you want for them?" my dad asked the breeder.

"Two hundred fifty for the males and $300 for the females," she answered.

"Is there any dog you like more than the other?" Dad asked Michael and me.

"No, not really," I said, "they're all about the same."

"Yeah, but I really think we should go with a girl," Dad said.

It was then I realized we were about to buy a dog. Dad reached into his pocket, pulled out his wallet, and produced three crisp one-hundred-dollar bills. Just like that, we had a new pet.

The new puppy rode home in Michael's lap in the backseat. I sat next to them. It was her first convertible ride, and she seemed thrilled to climb up Michael's chest and stick her head into the streamline of the wind zipping over the top of the windshield. All I could see was my brother's hands wrapped around her shoulders and the dog's big floppy ears smacking Michael about his glasses and the temples of his forehead. It looked like puppy nirvana. Then I thought of the hell that awaited us when we got home.

"Hey, Dad," I yelled over the sound of heavy 309 traffic and the strong wake of the wind, "how do you think Mom's going to take this?"

"Well, I don't know. She's on an all-women shopping trip right now, so we'll have a couple of hours before she comes back. Your guess is as good as mine. How do you think she'll like it?" he asked.

"I don't think she'll like it at all. Can you bring the dog back if Mom freaks out?"

"No. The $300 is nonrefundable. I just couldn't take it anymore. I needed another dog. Didn't you?"

"Yes."

"Well, let's just take her home. Hopefully, when Mom comes back she sees how cute the dog is and falls in love with her. Then we won't have to send her back," Dad said.

BOB

Yeah I said that. What I remember most about the ride home from the breeder was frequent looks back in the rearview mirror to see my sons with our new dog. I felt old in wisdom, but young at heart. I remembered all the dogs I'd had, and all the dogs I'd lost. I remembered the joy of my father bringing home a new dog and the excitement of starting over. Here it is again, unfolding in my backseat. Whether it was the wind, or my emotions, I clearly remember tears filling my eyes and clouding my vision.

KEVIN

We dropped another $75 to $100 at a pet store on the way home, picking up chew toys, a small chain collar, and a pink leash.

"What about a name? I got a few names to consider," I told Dad as Michael and the puppy played next to me.

"Oh no. I've already named her. We're going to call her Susan Marie."

"What? We are? What kind of name is that for a dog?" I protested.

"No, no, no," Dad said having none of it, "I always liked the name Susan Marie. Since I have no daughters to name, she'll be my Susan Marie. You can call her Susie though."

Susie it was, and come to think of it, it was a pretty good dog name. When we pulled into the driveway, Susie jumped over onto my lap, extending her front paws to the top of the leather seat. She looked around at the trees and back at me. Then she tinkled right in my lap.

"Oh God!" I howled. "We were almost there!"

Hopping out of the car with her new pink leash attached, Susie lowered her nose to a millimeter off the pavement and zigzagged her way to the backyard. Behind the basketball hoop she found a twig and shredded it instantly.

"Make sure she goes to the bathroom before you bring her inside," my dad instructed. "We don't want to have an accident."

"Really, Dad? Look at me. Like I'm worried about her having an accident, after she already had had one on me."

That brought a quick laugh from my dad and brother. For a moment, I thought Mike might wet his pants too. It would only get better. Once we got inside, Susie got nosy again, leading herself in the direction of the kitchen where she found Danielle's old water/food combo bowl that was set out for her. She pushed it around on the linoleum floor. Figuring she wanted some water, I filled the bowl up.

She promptly jumped in and started a splash party. With more water on the floor than inside the bowl, she started steering the bowl around again. She didn't take a sip with the first offering I made, so I chose not to give her another. Eventually she moved on.

With wet paws, Susie left a trail from the kitchen to the living room. To understand our concern about what could go wrong in there, it's important to understand how paranoid my mother was about people—let alone a dog— wandering into her living room. The front of the room was okay for visitors, but Mom wouldn't let anyone in the back half where her prized, white down-feather couches sat cheeks-free, 364 days a year. She'd only allow us to sit on them on Christmas. Susie went right for the couches and started tearing at a dust ruffle.

"No, Susie!" I shouted.

Susie looked back with a why-not tilt of the head. From there she went over to Mom's polished work desk abutting the front of the living room and the foyer near the front door. The desk was more ornamental than functional. Susie promptly started gnawing on the leg of a wooden chair. In trying to nudge her away with my foot, she found my shoelaces equally delicious. It was a destructive sixty seconds since her big homecoming, but it was impossible to be angry with Susie because her face wouldn't allow it. She was too cute, too innocent looking. Her looks just didn't square with her behavior. The predictable squirts on the carpet would come later. They just weren't done with the same kind of pizzazz as the ones on her first day.

Like most puppies, Susie's bursts of energy were short lived. She followed them up with comatose naps that could take place anywhere, anytime. Her first nap in our house was on Dad's loafers—the ones on his feet. She just parked herself on top of his Florsheims as he stood in the doorway. She curled up in a ball, took a big yawn, closed her eyes and was fast asleep within seconds. Dad was looking around with an expression of "What do I do now?" He was between the kitchen and the stairs leading up to the bedrooms. There was really nowhere to go.

"Dad, don't move," I told him, "you might scare her."

He listened and didn't budge for the better part of fifteen minutes. He was starting to fidget and laugh uncomfortably. It was clear he couldn't hold still much longer.

Then the phone rang. Brrrrinnnggg! Brrrinnnggg! The call woke Susie up and did Dad a favor by allowing him to move his legs and shake out the cramps. Then he heard the voice on the other end.

Mike, Chris, Carole, and Kevin Walsh, 1989, with Susie at Christmas

BOB

"Hi, Carole, we're fine. We're just about to call Lorenzo's for a pizza. Everything's fine, everything's fine."

Susie seemed very interested in the conversation and moved in for a closer look. As my dad asked my mom for details of her shopping trip with friends, Susie started to climb the yellow stepstool, which doubled as a high chair. Woof, woof! she yelped.

"What is that I hear?" Mom asked loudly enough to be heard by Kevin and Michael through the receiver.

"Oh nothing," I told her.

Woof, woof, woof went Susie again followed by whining whimpers.

"That's not a dog I hear, is it?" Carole asked even louder than the first time.

Woof, woof, woof, woof. Susie continued trying to hijack the conversation.

At this point it was laughable, but I was trying not to laugh into the phone because that would have given it away completely. I didn't want to give Carole a chance to marinate in resentment on her ride home, but in my heart of hearts, I'm sure she knew what she was walking into. She'd heard the barking and the squeals, but couldn't see what they were coming from. Considering our past family history and love for dogs, she had to have known what was up.

KEVIN

A few minutes after her phone call, Mom's two-tone, dark and light brown Chevy Caprice pulled into our driveway on George Road in Meadowbrook. We weren't sure whether to bring Susie to the door for the maiden greeting or let Mom walk inside and discover her. We chose the latter.

I didn't want to let the dog out of the house, because it might give Mom a chance to tell her to "stay out." We blocked Susie inside the kitchen with eighteen-inch-tall wooden barriers that Dad had made for Danielle. They fit into slots that Dad installed on each side of the kitchen's doorways. The barriers were tall enough to keep a small dog from jumping over, but not so tall that a human couldn't step over.

Our previous dog, Danielle, would often stand on her hind legs and lift her front paws to the top of the wood. That would give her a view of the other side. Susie had yet to learn the trick.

Mom popped her trunk open revealing a collage of colored shopping bags. It looked as if Peddler's Village, a campy shopper's paradise in Bucks County, followed her home. We all grabbed as many bags as we could while Mom badgered us with questions about what we did while she was gone.

"We just kind of hung out," I told her as Michael and Dad chuckled.

"Come on guys, what's really going on?" Mom asked, clearly suspecting we were deflecting.

"You'll see," Dad said.

"See what?" she wanted to know.

And with that we entered the house and saw a happy face looking back at us from the top of the steps in the kitchen. It was Susie. She had her front paws on the edge of the wooden barrier and was looking over. That didn't take long to learn. When Susie saw Mom, her tail wagged and her dark eyes twinkled.

Mom looked at Dad in horror. Dad put his hands in his pockets and shrugged. I looked at Susie and she just looked like she owned the place.

"Mom, you have to admit, she's really cute isn't she?" I asked.

"Well she does have a cute face, but we'll have to see about her behavior."

And with that Susie peeled back from the barrier and piddled on the floor. What's more, she walked through her own puddle and pranced about the place with wet paws.

"Not a good start," Mom said.

Susie would grow fast in height and girth. She would eat anything, including vegetables. She housebroke easily, loved to take walks, and was a joy to fellow walkers who always seemed to want to pat her head. She loved attention and enjoyed watching people and nature go by.

Susie's most interesting quirk wasn't so much what she did but what she didn't do. After her first day with us, Susie never barked. It was nice because it kept the noise level down, but it didn't do much for security. We joked that if a robber came, we'd probably never know it. What's more, Susie might even help him find the jewelry. She absolutely did not have an aggressive bone in her body.

Within a few months I'd be off to college—leaving most of the dog-raising duties to Michael. He was hardly a rookie, but he'd never been a starter. Mom still thought his age was a nonstarter for such an upgrade in responsibility, but Dad and I more or less filibustered to the point that she didn't want to fight it.

"All right—whatever. But it's your dog. Don't ask me for any help when you guys are not around. I still don't think it's a good idea," Mom said.

Mom was just blowing off steam and was sticking it to us for bringing Susie home without her knowledge and blessing. We weren't worried. Mike was more than willing to play lead dog with the dog caretaking roles. He'd done well with Danielle, and there was no reason for us to believe he couldn't handle Susie. He did great and Dad helped when he could. Mom's concerns about it really were a nonissue.

Bob Walsh with brothers and sisters, Dick, Joyce, Cre, Jack Hall, Boots Walsh Hall, Albert, Jr., Bob, and Carole Walsh, 1990

BOB

Susie helped hold the family together when much of our idyllic lifestyle was changing. Carole had suffered a couple of sporadic seizures dating back to 1986. By 1990, they were becoming more regular. An MRI in the spring of 1990 revealed a mass inside her brain. Right around the Easter holiday she had cranial surgery to remove it. It was found to be a relatively low-stage malignancy, a stage two tumor. We were hopeful that it wouldn't come back, but with cancer you never know.

On top of that I changed jobs, accepting a position with the Pfizer Pharmaceutical Company in its Research and Development Division. With two kids in college, a sick wife, a young son, and a growing dog at home, there was a lot going on. A move from Meadowbrook, Pennsylvania, to southeastern Connecticut made a tough period in life even tougher.

The relocation was a tremendous blow to the family because we had never moved. I could have lived in my house on George Road forever. Carole and the kids felt the same. Susie, God bless her, couldn't have cared less.

The bad economy also killed the real estate market. Our house sat on the market for months. With Pfizer needing me up north, I relocated to Connecticut to start my new job, leaving Carole and Michael behind in Pennsylvania. Chris and Kevin were off at college. I found a nice little rental house in Niantic. It was a short commute to Pfizer on the Groton waterfront. The land was pretty and the new job was challenging, but I really missed my family. Used to coming home to the controlled chaos and cacophony of family, and then suddenly coming home to silence, it's deafening. I'd call every night, but it just wasn't the same.

I was commuting back to Meadowbrook each weekend, and the drives were long and tough. Depending on traffic, the drive ranged from five to seven hours. Squeezing around New York City traffic on either the George Washington Bridge or the Tappan Zee Bridge farther west by White Plains was always a crap shoot. At least I knew what was awaiting me on the other end. Susie would be waiting at the door with her tail wagging, stirring up a cloud of loose hair that lifted off her golden body. When she'd duck out to fetch me a gift of love—usually a sock or a shoe—Michael and Carole would step in with hellos and love of their own.

Sundays were always tough. There was the goodbye to family, followed by the grind of a long drive back to Connecticut in silence. I'd discovered books on tape, but really there's no substitute for a live body riding shotgun. Eventually, I filled that void with Susie.

Susie in Jeep, 1990

Susie was a great traveler. She'd just plunk herself down on the front seat and enjoy the ride. She even liked books on tape. When the music and narrator's voice took on an urgent tone, Susie would edge closer in her seat to the stereo speakers. She'd look up at me with a sense of wonder, or concern, fishing for reassurance that she was generating the appropriate response for what she heard. "Good girl, Susie," I'd say while stroking her head and making happy faces at her.

Where many dogs clamor about the window, pressing their noses against the glass, or trying to stick their heads out to catch the breeze, Susie didn't do that much. She was happy to sit back and chill. She took in the scenery, content to just let the world pass her by. Her world was where I was. She focused on me like I was a good date. She was a great companion and wonderful listener. Of course, she couldn't converse back, but sometimes you need a good listener more than anything else. Susie was the best.

Susie was even better at home. She brought new energy and appropriate cheer to a place that needed it. She woke up each day with a purpose to please. She gave so much love and companionship yet needed but a fraction of both in return. It was a simple life in which habit and ritual were repeated each day. She never tired of it.

Each morning I'd take her out for a brief walk. She'd do her business and sniff about to see who else did the same thing. She preferred the taller grasses near fence corners and edges that escaped the mower and weed whacker. We'd come home, have something to eat, and then prepare for the day ahead. For Susie that meant a day of rest; for me, a day of work.

Susie's day, I guess you could say, started earlier than mine. As I showered, shaved, and dressed for work, Susie was already resting on a bathmat inhaling the hot, steamy air. I'd step out of the shower and there she was looking at me in my glory. I'd plug in my electric razor and click it on, sparking the "snap" sound of the round blades, which hummed after twenty-four hours at rest.

I'd angle my gaze in the mirror to see Susie's reflection. Her eyes locked in on mine with a gentle focus. I'd finish and turn around for inspection. "How do I look, Suz?" I asked while jutting my chin forward and rubbing the smooth skin with my other hand. She'd lift one eyebrow and then the other. I don't know if that meant I looked so-so, but it was reaction worth seeing.

I'd put on my underwear, undershirt, dress shirt, and tie. Susie's gaze followed me the whole way. Only when I was fully dressed and reached for my briefcase would she finally return to her feet. She'd walk me to the door for the morning goodbye. "You be a good girl, Susie," I'd say before patting her on the head and heading out for work.

Sometimes I'd come home for lunch and Susie was thrilled. She'd greet me when I'd arrive, with a wagging tail and a grin on her face. Then, ever the Retriever, she'd bolt away to retrieve a gift. She never came back empty handed or, in her case, without something in her mouth.

Being that she was home all day usually meant Susie had to go to the bathroom right away when I'd come home. If I was up for it, we'd take a walk too. But if I was tired from the rigors of the day, Susie had no problem kicking back and relaxing. She was such a hang-out dog and made life alone much more tolerable.

After several months of vehicular weekend commuting and home sale hell, I got some good news from my company. It offered to buy our house in Pennsylvania. It was a wonderful gesture and the vehicle that would bring our family back together soon.

In searching for a new home though, Susie was starting to get the shaft. So when Kevin offered to bring Susie with him to live in his fraternity house at Purdue University in Indiana, I thought it would be another adventure for her.

KEVIN

Susie's higher education was an adventure, it's true, and it started before she got to campus. I drove home from Indiana one weekend in 1989 to get her. That's no short turnaround. It is 750 miles each way. I ditched class on a Friday and hit the road by mid-morning. By opening up the Dodge 600 on the open roads, I was able to shave about an hour and a half off the usual twelve-hour trip. I pulled into our driveway in Meadowbrook, Pennsylvania, right around dinner time and had Grandma's Chicken with Mom and Michael.

Dad would be coming down from Connecticut later that night with Susie and her dog supplies. That gave me a chance to go out and catch up with old acquaintances. I was one of just a few people in my extended circle of friends who went to college far away from home. My buddies made it a point to cancel their dates that night, or they brought their dates along to see me. Of course, they all wanted to know why I came home, as it wasn't a holiday weekend.

"Oh I'm just here to pick up my dog and bring her back to college with me," I told them.

"Hold on! You drove all the way home to pick up your dog? How long did that take?" Gary Bisaquino asked.

"About ten and a half hours," I said.

"Where's she going to live?"

"She's going to live in my fraternity house."

"Really? That sounds a little crazy. Are you sure that's a good place for her?"

"I think it'll be okay. We have a couple of other dogs that live in the house and they do just fine. Susie finds fun and happiness everywhere she goes."

Little did I know how a comment over a Corona could turn out to be so prophetic. After a couple of hours out with the guys, I went home. Later that night Dad rolled into our house with my new roommate. I hadn't seen Susie or my dad for a couple of months, so we had a good time catching up. Dad was melancholy about parting with Susie, but with having to move Mom and Michael up north, he had other things to focus on.

"Where will she stay in your house?" Dad wanted to know. "Will she only stay in your room?"

"Oh no, no, no. She'll probably sleep in my room, but she'll have the run of the house during the day."

"The guys you live with are okay with that?" he asked.

"Yeah, I brought it up during our Chapter meeting. I told everyone she was housebroken and very obedient. It's not a problem. We have a couple of other dogs at the house, but Sparkles and Dillon aren't really big into socializing. Susie's going to have a grand time."

"Does she have a place to go to the bathroom?" Dad wanted to know.

"Yes, we have a pretty big lawn around the house, so there are plenty of places for her to go to the bathroom."

The next day I loaded the trunk with a forty-pound bag of Eukanuba Chicken and Rice Adult Dog Formula, a couple of leashes, a doggy bed, and Susie's stainless steel food bowls. I put Susie in the backseat, but as soon as we got out of the driveway, she climbed up front, and curled up in the front seat. It was clear she'd done this before. By the time we got to the Pennsylvania Turnpike, and I was merging into the fast lane, I looked over and saw Susie fast asleep.

We stopped for gas and food a few times, and the mandatory doggie breaks when nature called. It was a smooth ride that ended eleven hours later. As I pulled into the chewed-up parking lot of the Pi Kappa Alpha house, I could see, hear, and feel the pulsating vibrations of a kicking party in progress. Before heading in, I took Susie to the side lawn of the house so she could go to the bathroom. She found someone who had the same thing in mind, mistaking bushes on the corner of West Stadium and University Avenues for a toilet. Not shy about anything, Susie moved in for a closer look. It startled the young man who finished up fast and patted Susie's head.

"I like your dog," he said, while zipping up.

"Thanks. Find a bathroom next time," I told him.

"You got it," he said with a laugh.

After that we were off to join the fun inside. Susie was a hit the second she walked through the door. "Awwwwww," the girls cooed, "who is this dog?"

"It's Susie," I told them.

"She is so cute!"

I could hardly make it to the stairs that led to the upper floors of the house. Everyone—and I mean everyone—wanted to pet the dog. Susie was beaming, beaming! A half-hour later I still hadn't unpacked the car, and I was badly in need of a beer after a long drive. Eventually, one of the brothers said, "Gimme the dog. I'll bring her upstairs. Go get your stuff out of the car."

So I handed the leash over and watched as he walked directly over to a huddle of pretty coeds. What a dog, I thought! He's using my dog to pick up chicks. Really, though, it was funny, and come to think of it, previously, he wasn't too successful with the ladies. I don't know what it led to, but he was off to a good start in their eyes.

I fetched my stuff from the car and brought it up to my room on the third floor next to the stairwell. Then I went in search of Susie who, by the time I found her, was off leash and frolicking about with foam around her mouth. I later found out what the foam was from when I saw her dunk her muzzle into a plastic Solo cup filled with beer. Susie had joined the party in spirit and spirits.

"Susie, no!" I shouted.

Susie took her snout out of the drink and rushed to my side with tentative pitter patter steps, lowering her head in shame. Knowing she let me down, she sat down on my right side and looked up with the sorriest of eyes and droopy ears. It is moments like this that make dogs my pet of choice. They get it. They know when they've disappointed us, and they are crushed by it. The trouble is, sometimes they have short memories.

I couldn't hold a grudge for long, and it wasn't long before Susie wandered off and made more friends. "Oh!" I heard a girl squeal from a room in which Susie entered. "Who is this dog? Oh she's so cute!"

I just followed the voices to the room of two brothers who were hosting some well-dressed ladies from the Kappa Kappa Gamma sorority. Susie was lapping up the attention and the libations being served. She graduated from keg beer to some kind of jungle juice in a decorated plastic tumbler, all in the course of about five minutes.

All the fussing over Susie whipped up a storm of golden hair, which either stuck to the dark dresses or landed in the drinks. Based on the girls' pace of consumption, I'm fairly sure they didn't know they consumed a few hairballs in the effort.

Realizing a familiar theme was unfolding with Susie and her zest for life and libations, I took what I thought would be a preventive measure to curb her drinking from places other than her water bowl. I found an old nametag clip-on. It was a leftover from a rush party at our house. I took the paper out of the sleeve and flipped it over. With a black Sharpie I wrote: "No booze for Suz." I clipped it on the top of her collar. It was big enough that it drew attention and forced a closer look. The words were an introduction and an instruction. I felt good about the effort and gave Susie some space.

What I didn't imagine was how counterproductive the message would turn out to be. If anything it encouraged more drinking. Seeing that her indulgences only amounted to a lick or two, I didn't think it would be that big of a deal.

Later that night after the party broke up, and people either went home or to bed, I saw Susie walking down the long hallway of the fraternity house's third floor. She could not have walked more crooked. It was clear she was smashed. I got her into my room and she folded like a cheap tent. She was out, and she snored—all night.

The next morning I woke up to the sound of Susie whimpering by the door. She had to go outside. I dressed as fast as I could, but not fast enough. Before we even got out of my room, she soiled the rug. This was no easy clean up, and it wouldn't be a one-time affair. Susie had a taste for the hooch. The enablers were plenty, and so were the episodes in which she'd stumble back to my room in the sauce.

Seeing your dog wasted is funny—once. After that, it's just too much work. I can't tell you how many times I'd hear a knock on my door in the morning. "Walsh! Your dog went to the bathroom in the living room! Come clean it up."

It got old real fast. So did the wanderlust. Even when Susie didn't have to go potty, she'd position herself by the front door, knowing at any moment any one of my eighty fraternity brothers might be coming in. When that door opened, she was out and off to explore. How she was never hit by a car at the busy intersection right in front of the fraternity house, I'll never know. There were plenty of close calls though.

One fall day I was returning from class and walking on the mall by the fountain. The weather was warm and students were lounging about on the grass and on the walls. Out of the corner of my eye I saw a white flash followed by a golden one. The white flash was a Frisbee. The golden one was my dog chasing it.

"Hey, that's my dog," I said to the Frisbee tosser.

"You know she's been out here for the last three hours and was drinking out of the fountain?" he said more in the form of a scold than a question.

"Well, no, I didn't know that," I said with a sarcastic laugh, "but it doesn't surprise me."

I took Susie home and she slept for the rest of the day. Whether it was playing Frisbee, drinking from the fountain, visiting Ross Ade Stadium, or trespassing on the school's golf courses—Susie got around. Searching for the new Purdue mascot was almost becoming a daily occurrence.

About a month after the Frisbee Olympics, I returned to the fraternity house to find Susie missing once again. I walked around the corner and started down Waldron Street. By the time I reached the four hundred block, I noticed a familiar sight—pretty girls crowding around a familiar dog. Susie was on her back getting a belly rub from the ladies at Chi Omega. She was thrilled and so were the girls. Attached to her collar was a rope in the form of a leash. Holding the rope was a nice young man who looked about my age. He had a handle on the situation.

"Hi," I said to him, "you found my dog. Thanks for taking care of her. Where did you find her?"

"Well, I live at the Sig Eps house. I was in my room doing homework, and she came walking right in like she knew where she was going. She plopped down on the floor and fell asleep. I didn't think much about it because we have a few house dogs already. I just figured somebody else brought their dog from home and now we had another one. But after an hour nobody came by looking for her. So I checked her tags and saw she was from Pennsylvania. I called your vet and left a message. Then I called your house and talked with your dad. You may want to check in with him."

"Yeah, I will. Hey, thanks a lot. I really appreciate you taking good care of her," I said while shaking his hand. "By the way, what's your name?"

"My name is Kevin Walsh," he answered.

"What is your name?" I asked again, thinking I may have misheard him, but astonished to hear what sounded familiar.

"Kevin Walsh," he said.

"You're kidding me," I said with a sense of wonder that he didn't quite understand, but was curious about.

"No, I'm not. Why?" he wanted to know.

"That's my name too. My name is Kevin Walsh."

"Oh my God!" he said, looking at me like he'd either seen a ghost, or couldn't believe his ears.

So to put this in proper context, my dog somehow managed to find the other Kevin Walsh on the campus of 40,000 students. How she got into that house, I'll never know. Why she went to the second floor, that's a mystery too. Not only did Susie find Kevin Walsh #2, the way he described it, she chose his room like there was no other option. It was as if she knew that was exactly where she was supposed to be.

BOB

I remember getting that phone call. A young man on the line said, "I found your dog in Indiana. Would you like her back?"

I said of course. Later my Kevin Walsh called and explained how Susie found the other one. I still can't quite believe it.

Bob gets the call. Susie is found!

KEVIN

Well, Susie's wanderings make for a great story, but at this point I was growing tired of the day-to-day searches for her. I worried about her safety. How much longer could I depend on the kindness of strangers, and even those with the same name to take good care of Susie when she got out of the house? The thought that the dog catcher or campus police would someday take her to the pound weighed on me too.

After careful thought I decided it was best to bring Susie home. It would be Thanksgiving in a couple of weeks. That would leave plenty more chances for Susie to study the blades of grass in front of President Beering's office window, visit tailgaters on Slater Hill during football games, take walks along the Wabash River, and of course to party like a rock star.

The Wednesday before Thanksgiving quite a few brothers stopped by my room on the third floor to say goodbye to Susie. She knew something was up. Her heavy eyes and droopy mouth corners gave her away. As I loaded up the car in the back parking lot, I saw her in the window looking down at me with the saddest face.

"Come on, Suz," I said when I went up to get her.

Susie lifted her muzzle, flared her nostrils and took a couple of whiffs of the air. I thought she was inhaling the memories of the good times she'd had with me at college. I couldn't help myself and I thought I'd reminisce too, while breathing deeply through my nose. I soon realized Susie wasn't reflecting—she was reacting.

A foul smell had quickly filled the room. She reached out and touched my foot with her front paw, looking up at me with a mischievous look. It was then I realized where the smell was coming from. She had had an accident, and I was standing right in the middle of a large pile of poop.

It was too funny to get upset about. I cleaned up the rug and scrubbed the sole of my shoe. The setback set us back about fifteen minutes. While I cleaned, Susie preened. She had to have known she got me good.

When it was really time to go, Susie climbed into the car, curled up shotgun, and rested her head on the armrest. I stroked her golden head as we headed east on Stadium Avenue and past the golden arches of McDonald's. She lifted her head for a last look and a sniff. We turned left on Northwestern Avenue, passing Boiler Bookstore on the right and Mackey Arena on the left. A minute later, we were off campus. I looked up and saw the Purdue University sign in the rearview mirror. Then I looked down and saw Susie sound asleep, probably dreaming of the good times she had had at a learning institution that was far more fun than obedience school.

Sans dog, I had more time on my hands to pursue things like dating. Luck struck fast. I met my future wife at a fraternity party. I saw her on the other side of a very crowded room. On the way over to chat, she disappeared. One of her friends, a Tri Delta sorority sister, gave me her name. I found the elusive gal a few minutes later. I went over and said, "Hi, Jean, I'm Kevin Walsh."

Jean Walsh, wife of Kevin Walsh, Wellesley, Mass., 2011

It was an instant connection. We've been together ever since. Jean has blessed me abundantly with love, companionship, a sense of adventure and best of all—

two equally beautiful daughters. And, as luck would have it, my wife has grown to love dogs too.

As for Susie, she would settle back into family life in Philly for just a couple of months. Later she would make the move with Mom and younger brother Michael to join Dad in Connecticut. Susie made the most of her time left in Philadelphia by visiting as many places and people as she could. Considering her propensity for doing the same when she was at Purdue, she really just picked up where she left off.

My older brother Chris was a senior at Villanova University, on the Main Line of Philadelphia. Villanova was just a half-hour drive from our home in Meadowbrook, so even though Chris was away, there were plenty of reasons to come home from time to time. Each time he came home, Susie was waiting for him, with cheer in her heart and always a new bandana wrapped around her neck.

During the Christmas break Chris worked at Wilburger's, a local ski shop with four locations around Philadelphia and the Greater Delaware Valley. His job involved a lot of driving. We all know how boring that can be, so to spice it up he brought Susie along.

CHRIS

I drove the daily delivery truck among four stores in Abington, Bryn Mawr, and Montgomeryville, Pennsylvania, and the Wilmington, Delaware, store. It was about four hours round-trip, plus load time. The van had a state-of-the-art stereo system and I wasn't stuck inside all day. But that got old real quick with traffic and boredom. Susie was the perfect solution, but I couldn't let Mike, the owner, know she was riding with me. In order to keep that from Mike, I took an alternate route back to the house on George Road to pick up my happy passenger, before setting out for each day's journey.

Usually Mom would have Susie waiting at the back door with her snazzy neckwear. Susie was always excited to go to work. Mom wasn't particularly fond of the dog, but she put that aside when she got Susie and her bandanas ready. Maybe it was a girl thing, and she wanted Susie to look pretty, or maybe Mom just knew how much Susie meant to us.

Susie meant a lot to a lot of other people too. She was an instant hit with folks along the route. People would wave and call out her name: "Susie!" She absolutely loved it. Employees and customers at the sites loved Susie's spirit, and especially her bandanas.

The only person who didn't know what was up was my boss Mike. We had to keep it that way. Often we'd get word that Mike was headed to the store, so we would scramble to hide Susie, or hit the road before his arrival. Our plan worked without a hitch until one weekend when Mike decided to take the van out on a business lunch. Seems the sheepskin seat-covers were a magnet for dog hair! Mike was wearing dark pants and a dark shirt and was covered from top to bottom in long "golden" dog hair.

The confrontation between Mike and me was hilarious. He looked ridiculous and in need of a lint roller.

"Chris, where did all this dog hair come from?" he asked.

It was hard to answer because I was laughing so hard. "Well, driving all day is boring. So I thought I'd bring my dog along to make it more interesting."

Mike took it well, but it was clear Susie had taken her last ride. It was great while it lasted. Susie had made a ton of friends along the way.

KEVIN

A few months after Susie's delivery job ended, it was time for her next journey in a new place. Dad found a lovely white colonial house with red shutters in the wooded Parsonage Hill section of Ledyard, Connecticut. The family moved north to join him in September 1990. The house was located on a two-and-a-half-acre corner lot, surrounded by non-buildable conservation land. It was bucolic and very New England.

There was an abundance of wildlife, which made for good nature watching. Deer lived in the woods behind the house. Sometimes while doing the dishes we could look out the window and see a white-tailed doe with fawns trekking through the trees and brush. Birds were plentiful and were attracted to our backyard feeders. Occasionally we'd be treated to a male cardinal's visit. Resplendent in red and proud in presentation, the cardinal never had to wait to eat. The less attractive sparrows and robins moved aside respectfully. The cardinal took what he wanted, and did so with regal grace.

The squirrels knew no such grace. They, in fact, were a royal pain in the rear. They chased our cardinal friend away and every other bird too. You always knew when the squirrels arrived because, in an instant, the birds disappeared. The squirrels would shimmy down the tubular feeder hanging from a tree branch and eat upside down. They did it with an incredible feat of balance, and impossibly sharp claws on their feet. They'd gorge themselves for up to an hour at a time.

Susie took the squirrel invasion as a personal affront. Even though she almost never barked, you could see the agitation come over her. Susie would shake and paw at the glass door, which led to the back deck. Quietly I'd open the door and point to a spot behind the gas grill that offered cover. Then I'd whisper with urgency, "Go get 'em, Suz!"

Bob, Carole, and Michael with Susie, 1990

Susie would scurry down the wooden steps to the grass below. The sound of her hustling down the steps acted as a heads up to the squirrels. The squirrels would let go of the feeder, crash to the ground, and furiously scamper away just ahead of Susie's gnashing teeth. She never did catch one, but she always gave them a heckuva scare.

Susie also seemed to take to the new home as a new opportunity to connect with Mom. Sadly, Mom was having a tough time and a recurrence of cancer in early 1991. The tumor that had been removed from her brain a year prior was back and growing fast. Her aggressive treatment involved chemotherapy that made her very nauseated and weak. Susie would move in to try to help, but more often than not she'd get in the way. Susie was undeterred. She never stopped trying to show Mom her love, and Mom, by now, had grown to appreciate it.

It wouldn't be much longer until doctors determined Mom would need a second surgery to remove the growth on her parietal lobe. The procedure was done in July 1991. The tumor was twisted and difficult to remove. It left Mom paralyzed on the right side of her body, and largely bedridden. That's not all.

The malignancy had changed from stage two to stage four—the most aggressive kind of cancer. Susie never left Mom's side. She often put herself under the at-home motorized hospital bed, which could be moved up and down with the touch of a button. More than once we almost crushed Susie when we lowered the bed. It became standard operating procedure—look for the dog before you lower the bed.

One September day Mom's limp arm fell through the safety railing of her bed. Seeing that Mom was struggling and unable to do anything about it, Susie lifted Mom's hand with her head. She flipped it gently over the bedrail. It was such a tender moment that provoked profound words.

"You're a good dog, Susie," Mom said barely able to turn her head enough to look into Susie's longing eyes.

They were Mom's final words to Susie. We took Mom to the hospice wing at Lawrence and Memorial Hospital in New London, Connecticut, the next day. A week later, she died just a couple of hours after my parents' wedding anniversary, and far too young at the age of fifty-one.

Susie came to the wake, which we held in Abington, Pennsylvania, so all of Mom's friends in her adopted hometown could attend. Susie sat proudly in Chris's blue Jeep outside the Baron Rowland Funeral Home, adorned with a red bow.

"Susie had earned the right to join in the funeral process," Dad said.

Plenty of folks asked about the dog on the way in, and plenty of them made sure to pet Susie on the way out.

Susie would live another year in the family home in Connecticut before doing what a lot of Nutmeggers and other folks in northern climates do in their golden years— move south. Chris had a new job with Merrill Lynch in

Jacksonville, Florida, and wanted to bring Susie along. With a bit of negotiating and some reluctance on Dad's part, Dad finally gave in. Susie was off on a new adventure to her fourth home.

BOB

Oh, it was so hard to see Susie go. She was such a good dog, and I had waited so long to give that name to someone I loved. So what if it was a dog? I loved her and I just adored the name Susan Marie. I loved what she did for my wife and what she meant to our family. I remember it like it was yesterday.

Christopher really needed a source of support for the new challenge ahead of him in a strange place far away from home. I couldn't see anything or anyone who would be there for him more than Susie could. She had a track record to prove it. As any parent knows, it's hard to see your children leave the nest. You're immensely proud that you've done your job in raising them well, so they can become self-sufficient. But when that day comes, it's like a part of you dies. You're not just saying goodbye to your child, you're saying goodbye to a major part of your life.

Having lost Carole to cancer less than two years previously, and seeing my son walk out the door—with my best friend no less—that was a lot to handle. Believe me, believe me, it all came together like a tornado. I couldn't think of a better gift to give to him than Susie to send him on his way. I'm not sure I ever felt better and worse at the same time.

CHRIS

I think I've seen my dad cry once, maybe twice in my life. He's not big on showing emotion, but I know he was crying inside. At the same time I realized how precious it was that he would let something he loved so much leave with me.

With Susie everything was an adventure. The movers came and loaded up the big truck. They drove my blue Jeep right into the back of the trailer and locked it down for the 1,100-mile drive south. Then Canine Carriers showed up in a marked white van. The plan was to put Susie in her crate, drive her to Newark, New Jersey, put her on a plane and fly her down to Florida. I was a little nervous about turning her over to strangers and not being on the same flight with her. But after watching her play with the van's driver on our front lawn for a half hour, I knew it'd be okay. He clearly loved dogs and Susie was comfortable with him.

The plan took a slight detour when it was time to load Susie into the crate. The driver asked, "Hey do you mind if she rides up front with me instead of in the crate?"

"No, not at all," I told him.

There was one catch. Susie would have to wear a seatbelt. It was funny to see her sitting in the front seat as the driver tried to get the shoulder harness across her chest and buckled into its slot. After several failed tries, Susie stopped resisting. She seemed to realize the alternative was to ride in the crate. From what I heard, she rode like a champ.

Susie was in a kennel for her first week in Jacksonville, as I hunted for a place to live. Once I found digs, I ditched everything and went over to get her. I missed her so much. When they brought her out, her tail was wagging so hard that it knocked over some small fixtures on the shelves in the waiting area. It was funny and flattering. Susie obviously missed me too.

Susie adjusted to her new life in a new place just like she always did—she owned it. I was lucky to have some friends living nearby, and Susie made friends with them instantly.

Chris with Susie on the beach in Florida, 1993

Among the friends were past pals from my lifeguarding days on Long Beach Island at the Jersey Shore.

One day Matt and Chris Juall offered to help me move furniture. Of course I was going to take the twins up on it. In return, I treated them to beers and hot dogs on the grill. I warned them not to leave their food unattended. Within seconds, they knew why. After preparing a piping hot hot dog, one of the brothers carelessly put his plate down and turned his head away. Susie inhaled the hot dog in fast fashion. But it was too hot to eat. We watched in horror/amusement as she regurgitated the hot dog and ate it three times over!

Other friends from New Jersey would become regular visitors too. One became a roommate. Mike Walsh, who's not related, called me out of the blue and said he'd had his fill of corporate America and was looking for a break. I invited him to come down. He didn't just visit, he moved in. We built a bunk loft in my one-bedroom apartment. He was great company and we shared expenses. The biggest benefactor was Susie. Susie had another pal to play with.

Mike was golden with Susie. He played with her all the time. He worked at a local gym and had a bit more flexibility to come home during the lunch hour. That was good for Susie's bladder and her disposition. She came to count on him and looked forward to his midday visits as much as anything.

Weekends were even better. Susie went everywhere we did, including the beach. This was a little dicey as dogs weren't allowed on the beach in Ponte Vedra. Nobody seemed to mind because we always cleaned up after Susie, and people flocked to her—especially children. Parents loved Susie because she helped their little children run off energy, while mom and dad relaxed and enjoyed the view.

Even if Susie was the dog version of the Pied Piper, this mattered little to the animal control officers whom we were often a step ahead of. One day, a stealthy pair managed to sneak up right behind us. We tried to conceal

Susie under a towel with a cockamamie story about how it was a sleeping friend. No dice. We left the beach that day with bad sunburns, a $75 ticket, and another great Susie story to tell.

In many ways, life was changing for me. Work was becoming busier and the days were longer. On top of that, I started dating Suzanne Finaldi. Suzanne was a good Jersey girl with blonde hair. We had a lot in common, including parents with New Jersey and New York connections. I'm not sure Suzanne liked Susie as much as she tolerated her.

The smell of a wet dog and dirty ears really freaked Suzanne out. Nevertheless, I think Suzanne came to accept the fact that Susie and I were a package deal. Susie sensed a change and figured out she was being pushed into the background. But in her usual good graces, Susie just accepted my relationship with Suzanne, and she worked on making Suzanne love her too.

More changes would come, which included my friend and roommate Mike moving back north, and my moving in with Suzanne at her house on Raley Creek Drive. Suzanne and I eventually married. Like most married couples we went about expanding our family. Not with kids just yet, but first with another dog. Suzanne had always wanted a small dog. I figured if she was good enough to let me and Susie in, we had to return the favor.

We brought home a little Shih-Tzu and named her Raley, after the street we lived on. There was no jealousy from Susie, and soon the two dogs were the best of friends. Raley, being smaller and more agile, would often bounce to and fro over Susie, as Susie relaxed on the cool floor tiles. On occasion when Susie had had enough, she would intercept Raley with a clothesline reaching paw, or the occasional nip. It was simply her mature way of saying no more.

Sadly, Raley wasn't blessed with the longevity Susie would come to know. She had a genetic kidney disorder that was poisoning her from the inside. Not wanting her to suffer, we made the agonizing decision to put Raley to sleep. It was especially rough on Suzanne because Raley really was her dog. In many ways Susie stepped up and comforted Suzanne as much as I did.

Other Shih-Tzus would follow, but Susie really was the mainstay of our family. In so many ways, she was our first child. We nursed her through hotspots, ear infections, and other illnesses. We watched her as she aged, her once golden snout turning a distinguished gray. As she aged, so did her role and responsibilities in our family.

Our first child, Tyler, was born in July 1996. As first-time parents, naturally we were concerned about Susie's reaction to the new addition. Would she be resentful?

Would she be aggressive? Similar to how Susie stood watch over Mom in her final days battling brain cancer, Susie quickly found her spot at the base of Tyler's crib and stood guard. There was a lot of comfort for both parties. We knew Tyler was under a watchful eye, and Tyler was always calmer in Susie's presence.

Tyler Walsh with Susie and Raley poolside, 2000

It was fun to watch Tyler and Susie together, and it was special to know that I was passing on to him a gift that my father had shared with me when I was a child—a love of dogs. It would only get better in time as Tyler would grow and expand the boundaries of his adventures with Susie by his side. As a toddler, Tyler would lie alongside

Susie on the ground and pat her head. Her soft brown eyes would look directly into his bright blue ones, setting off a reflection that warmed the soul.

When Tyler got older, playtime with Susie got more sophisticated. While slowly driving into our neighborhood development one day, my car was passed by a dog towing a redheaded kid on a skateboard. They looked familiar. When they turned into our driveway, I knew why. And that's how those two were—always happy, always playing.

Of course all the activity usually set up a need to cool off. There was nothing better than to jump into the pool on a steamy North Florida day. Susie took to the pool like a duck to water. It was a given she was going in. You would see two redheads working their way across the length of the pool: one was Tyler, the other was Susie.

Susie and Tyler were fine swimmers. Trouble was they often brought the pool inside the house with them. To Suzanne's dismay, Tyler and Susie's wet feet tracked a lot of dirt into the house. Oftentimes Susie would rub up against the white walls and leave half-moons of dirt behind. As much as our beloved animals often figure things out, make adjustments and just seem to eventually "get it," Susie never got the concept of treading lightly in the house when she was dirty. The dirt came off wherever she shook, rubbed, rolled, or walked. Why should she care? She didn't have to clean it up.

As she aged Susie began to develop a growth on the left side of her neck. We were concerned when we first noticed it and immediately brought it to the attention of our veterinarian, Dr. Michael Schumer. Having known us from the time we moved to Jacksonville, Dr. Schumer always provided the best of care to Susie. Because Suzanne and I had both lost loved ones to cancer, our initial fear was that cancer was back in our lives and taking hold of Susie's neck. The biopsy came back negative.

Although the growth was somewhat unsightly and fast-growing, Dr. Schumer advised us that Susie, who was then thirteen years old, was an otherwise happy and healthy dog. As time went on, the mass continued to grow and Susie began to lose weight. I remember speaking to my dad and assuring him that we had Susie under a doctor's care. We would not let her suffer.

Other problems developed, unrelated to the growth on her neck. She developed severe bouts of diarrhea, dehydration and she continued to lose weight. It was at that point that we decided that it was time. We would not let a dog that had given us so much suffer any pain.

I will never forget that day in 2002. Suzanne and Tyler said their final goodbyes to Susie and it's fair to say they were inconsolable.

"Come on, Suz. Let's go for a ride," I said as I attached her leash to her collar.

I opened the back door of our tan-colored Xterra and put her in the backseat. It was a short drive to the vet, but it seemed to take forever. I still remember the song that played on the radio that morning. I don't know the title, but I know the song and whenever I hear it now, I have to change the station.

I talked to Susie along the way too. I told her she was a good dog to me and the family, and I thanked her for that. I prayed as well. I think she knew something was up. How do I know? She just had a look on her face that said so. It was a sad look, but an accepting one. Her eyes looked heavy.

We hardly fussed once we got to the office. I think they do it that way—decisively—to get it over with quickly. It's probably just as well, but it really hurt. I held Susie in my arms and comforted her as my vet friend inserted the needle into the top of her back. She didn't struggle at all, and in just a few seconds the life in her body had left her.

I left the vet feeling as if I had swallowed an apple. The lump in my throat stuck around for a long time. When I got home, I could hardly speak. Nobody else could either. It was just a sad, sad time. But later we all agreed it was necessary, and we were lucky to have her as long as we did. We had no doubt she was in a better place and probably sitting by Mom's side wearing a pretty bandana. Those thoughts helped, but it still hurt, a lot.

EIGHT

Crazy Daisy Rules

BOB

In 1993, I was a widower. My son Michael was fifteen and a sophomore in high school. My other sons, Chris and Kevin, had recently graduated from college and were living their lives in different parts of the country and across the globe. It was just Michael and me in a big house. We had each other, but something was missing. Were we pathetic? No, I wouldn't say we were pathetic, but we were lonely. I missed having a dog and so did Michael.

We had a talk, which probably took place at the kitchen table. If it wasn't there it was in the den. The location really isn't as important as the content of the conversation. The bottom line was that we both wanted a dog.

Bob's son Michael Walsh, now thirty-four, has raised four dogs. His current dog is Georgia, a Doberman Pinscher mix.

MICHAEL WALSH

It's true we did. Things were tough after Mom died in 1991. Dad may have wanted me to have a dog because of other things too. I was fifteen and a good kid, but sometimes trouble just finds you. A serious car accident a few days before my dog talk with Dad left my face busted up pretty bad. My nose needed to be reset, and I took quite a few stitches in the chin. It was a horrible night that I remember well. The hospital called Dad and told him about the accident. They told him to bring a picture of me so the doctor would have an idea of what my face looked like before the crash. How would you feel getting such a call?

I can only imagine Dad's fear, walking into Lawrence and Memorial Hospital. The last time he was there was when Mom died. All he knows is that his son was in a serious car accident and he wouldn't know how bad it really was until he got there. The hospital wasn't going to give all the information over the phone. He was really shaken up when I saw him walking in and holding a framed picture of me in his hand. I'm sure he thought about Mom and the fact that he almost lost me as well. How lonely would that big house in Ledyard be if things didn't work out for me? I think getting a new dog was sort of his way to share something special with me, and maybe to protect himself.

BOB

A house like ours really screamed out for a dog and so did our hearts. Michael suggested a Dalmatian and I thought, why not? How can you not love those little spots? So I took out the *New London Day*, combed through the classifieds and wouldn't you know it? I spotted a litter of Dalmatian puppies available. The breeder was in

Danielson, Connecticut, about an hour away from our house. I called her and made an appointment.

Michael and I made the drive hoping we wouldn't come home with just the two of us. The breeder was a nice lady who was going through a tough time. She had cancer. She wanted to move the dogs fast. I don't know if it was because she needed the money, or was worried that something terrible might happen to her before she found homes for the dogs.

The dogs were just as cute as could be, and very playful. I watched Michael as he played with the bunch. Then I joined him in the fun. We plucked one from the litter which had good spots and a warm disposition. The breeder was thrilled with our decisiveness. We were happy to finally have a new friend to bring into our home.

I had already decided on a name. We would call the dog Daisy. It was Michael's first Daisy dog and my second. The name had nothing to do with honoring Daisy the Cairn Terrier, who wound up under the wheel of a passing car years before. The Dalmatian pup just looked like a Daisy.

By now it was my fourth ride home with a dog in my child's lap, but it felt as good as my first. Michael was glowing. So was Daisy. So was I. My heart did a dance just like it did when we brought home Daisy #1, Danielle and Susie. Michael may have been my youngest son, but he had a leg up on his older brothers in dog deliveries. Susie was his first lap dog car ride home. Daisy was the second. Chris and Kevin had just one of those rides a piece.

It was the first really good news Michael and I shared in quite some time. As I drove my car south on I-395, it wasn't lost on me that a dog once again was the vehicle that connected me to my family much like it had before, and like nothing else quite could.

"She's going to be a lot of fun, Dad," Michael said while looking up with a smile that lit up the highway.

I just grinned and nodded back.

The next day we took Daisy to our vet for a checkup. She got a clean bill of health. Housebreaking Daisy was surprisingly easy. Of course there were a few accidents and cleanups, but Daisy understood the concept of relieving herself outside faster than any other dog I knew. She just got it. She was completely housebroken in three days. And if we left her alone for several hours for whatever reason, she never had an accident—ever.

Daisy, 1996

Michael: *"Daisy was a chick magnet. There were a number of girls in the neighborhood who were interested in seeing my cute puppy, and they were girls I was interested in. That was part of the reason I wanted to get a Dalmatian. I admit it. You should have seen it when Dad took her to Mystic."*

Bob: *"She was an absolute chick magnet, but I didn't use her for that."*

Kevin: *"Oh c'mon, Dad, be honest!"*

Bob: *"No, no, no. I didn't!"*

I just loved to take her for walks in downtown Mystic, and Daisy loved it too. Downtown Mystic is a beautiful place to take a stroll. I'd walk down Main Street and all but start a parade. People would come running out of shops and stores to fawn over Daisy. Old women, young women, teenage girls, they couldn't get enough of her. I'm not sure that Julia Roberts walking down Main Street for a Slice of Heaven at Mystic Pizza could've created a bigger fuss.

Daisy loved the attention and handled it with grace. Occasionally she'd sneak a lick of someone's ice cream cone, or try to climb onto their lap if they squatted down to greet her—the latter would become a pattern and problem. Most dogs outgrow lap climbing. Daisy never did. It was cute when she was little, but she wouldn't stay little for long.

By the time Daisy was six months old she weighed close to sixty pounds. That's a load to have on your lap. It's neither comfortable for you, or her, but somehow she didn't get that. Other issues surfaced that made her lap addiction even more problematic.

It was right around the six-month mark that Daisy's obedience took a sudden turn for the worse. I first noticed it when I prepared her food bowl for dinner and called her name, "Daisy. Daisy."

She didn't come. "Daisy!" I shouted louder.

With no response, I went looking for her. I saw her lying down on the floor inside the laundry room, her head facing in the opposite direction. "There you are! Come, Daisy, it's time to eat."

It was clear she didn't hear me even though I was just a few feet away from her. She responded only after I walked up toward her head. She either felt the vibration of my footsteps on the ground or saw me in her peripheral vision. I don't know who was more startled by her reaction—me or her. But once I gestured with my hand, she followed me into the kitchen and ate her dinner.

Later in the night, I sat in a comfortable chair to read a book. Daisy joined me in the room, retiring on the rug about ten feet in front of me. Every few pages I'd look over the top of my reading glasses to check on her. Without being demonstrative, I called her name: "Daisy."

She didn't budge. Not even a flick of the ear or a tilt of the head. I did it again even louder. "Daisy!" I yelled.

Nothing, absolutely nothing. "Michael!" I called out.

Michael came downstairs from his room. "Yeah, Dad, what's up?" he asked while standing in the breezeway of the den.

"Has Daisy been responding to you when you call her name or tell her to do something?"

"Lately it's like she doesn't hear," he answered while shrugging his shoulders.

While listening to Michael I noticed Daisy looking directly at me. She didn't even realize Michael was right behind her talking loudly. It was obvious she couldn't hear at all. Our beloved dog was stone deaf. It was as if it happened overnight.

It wasn't just her hearing, her behavior changed drastically too. No longer could you give her soothing pats on the head or strokes down her back. If you touched her, simply touched her, she went crazy.

KEVIN

While Dad and Mike were managing the maniac that Daisy had become, I was busy trying to manage the third step in my budding television career. I was three years into a six-year stint in Fresno, California, and hadn't made it back to the East Coast in quite some time. Luck was on my side with the 2000 holiday vacation schedule, so I booked flights to Connecticut for Christmas. I guess I had forgotten what awaited me.

Before Dad could warn me, I made my way over to Daisy and patted her head. It was like flipping a switch. She went berserk. She nipped at my hands, boxed with her paws and tried to climb onto my lap despite the fact that I was standing.

I tried everything to get her to calm down, including turning my back, ignoring her and holding her tightly.

Nothing worked. Eventually I walked out of the room. Later I came back to see if a break from Daisy made a difference. It didn't. The pattern repeated itself when I petted her again. It was sad. I wanted to show her affection, but I couldn't deal with what she gave in return. It was too much.

BOB

That's how life with Daisy was. There was a disconnect. How many of us have ever had a dog that you couldn't touch? That's like being in love and not being able to kiss your partner. I didn't love Daisy any less. In fact, I may have loved her even more. I compensated for what was missing. I loved her from a distance. It was tough.

* * *

MICHAEL

It was more than tough. It was borderline out of control. Daisy turned into a wild animal while living inside our house. She was cute to look at, but that's all you could do—look at her. If you touched her, you might get hurt. We all like to look at alligators and mountain lions, but would you ever bring one of those into your house? I pretty much ignored Daisy after she got so wild. I don't feel very good about it, but what could you do? If you touched her, she went crazy. I think we just felt bad about how it all turned out.

BOB

I called a couple of obedience experts and trainers. When I told them I was dealing with a deaf Dalmatian, they wanted no part of it. So I was really stuck with what I could do. Daisy would usually lie down on the floor in a position where she would watch whatever I was doing. Sometimes she'd come over fishing for attention, but if you touched her, you'd regret it.

KEVIN

Here's a good example of that from Christmas 2000. Our family home in Ledyard was filled with extended family, many of whom had flown in from around the country. After my mom died, my father married a lovely widow named Mary McGrattan. *When Bob Met Mary* should be a movie.

Mary has six adult children. Combine that with Dad's three adult children and we are a real-life Brady Bunch family. There are twenty grandkids. Obviously the holidays can get wild. Add a crazy dog into the mix and there was no shortage of shrieking kids, all trying to get away from Daisy.

One time, and only one time, I saw Daisy acting normal after six months of age. This is the lone exception to the Crazy Daisy Rule. After we opened presents that Christmas Day, my stepsister, Dr. Mauria McGrattan, had managed to settle Daisy into a comfortable position alongside of her. Mauria is a veterinarian. Clearly she has a deep understanding of animals and how to handle them. Somehow, to the shock of everyone, Mauria had Daisy in the prone position. She had her left arm wrapped around the dog's torso and was calmly stroking Daisy's head with the other hand. Daisy just accepted it, and almost appeared to be boasting that she was worthy and capable of receiving such tactile attention.

Feeling as if we might have experienced a breakthrough, that Daisy might be "cured," I came over to see if I could pet her too. No sooner did I make contact with the dog's head, my hand was in her mouth and she was all over me. The wonderful moment was over. I never should have touched her.

Seconds later Daisy went right back to Mauria and plopped down alongside her. Mauria, you could say, had "the Touch."

BOB

I never thought about putting her down because of her condition. Not once. People ask me about it all the time. It wasn't her fault that she was the way she was. It was just too bad that I couldn't share more of myself with her, and I couldn't share her with other people after she reached the age of six months. It was like having had something special and then losing it. Gone were those nice walks through Mystic where Daisy was the main attraction.

Even if the total package that was Daisy wasn't so attractive anymore, I managed to attract the attention of

Mary McGrattan. Like me, she had lost her spouse about two years before. Mary actually met my wife just before we put Carole into hospice. We had to have some legal documents notarized before taking Carole to the hospice wing at Lawrence and Memorial Hospital in New London. Mary was then the Mayor of Ledyard, and a public notary.

KEVIN

I remember we went to city hall. Mom was too sick to make it inside. Mary graciously came outside with her notary embosser. She was very kind and meticulous, making sure that Mom was sound of mind and understood what she was signing.

"Carole, how are you?" Mary asked.

"Oh I'm doing the best I can, I guess," Mom answered.

"Carole, do you understand exactly what it is you're signing and what it means?"

"Yes."

Mary watched closely as Mom signed on a blank line. I could hardly read her name. If I hadn't seen Mom do it, I wouldn't have known it was her signature. It was so sad because I had never seen another signature as pretty as hers. Her penmanship had always been perfect—perfect, with long flowing lines and particular attention paid to the C in Carole and the W in Walsh. It was art.

Mary saw us off and her compassion wasn't lost on any of us.

"She was really nice, wasn't she?" Mom asked more in the form of a statement than a question as we drove to the hospital.

Bob Walsh and Mary McGrattan, 2011

"She sure was," Dad answered.

The next time I saw Mary was the day before she married my dad. I was overseas from 1993 to 1995, building my television news career in the U.S. Territory of Guam. I missed Dad and Mary's entire courtship. But I remember getting a call in the middle of the night on the other side of the globe with the news: "Hey, Kevin, guess what? I'm engaged," my dad said.

"Really? Anyone I know?" I asked.

"Actually, you do. It's Mary McGrattan, the former Mayor of Ledyard who notarized the papers before we took Mom to hospice. Mary went on to become a Connecticut State Representative. I was assigned to lobby her. We met at a political function," Dad explained.

That was quite a phone call to get at 3:00 a.m. Usually when the phone rings at that hour it's bad news.

BOB

Mary didn't remember me at the event, but I remembered her. I had to remind her of that moment at city hall with Carole and Kevin a couple of years before. We had a lot in common and we fell in love.

KEVIN

I was flying home from Guam for Dad and Mary's wedding in June 1995. I was on the last leg of a thirty-three-hour trip with five connections. On a Continental Express ATR-42 puddle jumper from Philadelphia to Providence, Rhode Island, I sat next to a rebellious teenage girl named Nicole. Nicole seemed very anxious. I asked her if she was afraid to fly.

"No it's not that," she answered with a sigh. "I'm just really nervous because my dad is picking me up at the airport."

"Why would you be nervous about that?" I asked curiously.

"Because I haven't seen him in almost ten years since he left the family."

Her answer caught me totally off guard. I wasn't prepared for such heft and what followed.

"He never called and never paid child support. I hate him for what he did to my mom and me," Nicole unloaded.

I was stunned and it showed. But I listened.

"So out of the blue my dad calls me up and asks if he can see me. I'm like, no way! Why now? He cried on the phone and said he was a coward for what he did. Now he wants me in his life? Why should I give him what he wants? I may tell him to f… off when I see him."

She poured her heart out to me, a total stranger.

"Wow! That's a lot to handle," I said, "and I can see how you feel the way you do. I think anyone would. Was he a good dad before he left?"

"Yeah, he was. He was really good."

"Do you think about the good times?"

"All the time."

"Do you miss those times?"

"Yeah I miss them a lot. He's missed so much of my life."

I needed to come up with something fast, something meaningful. I don't know where it came from, but pretty soon appropriate words were falling out of my mouth.

"You know something, honey? Maybe you want the same thing he does a do over. He probably tried to make that call years before, but didn't have the courage to pick up the phone. He admitted he was a coward. That's a tough thing for a man to do. Maybe you can help him become the man he was before, and the father you want back. Aren't you exhausted from years of hating him?"

"Oh yeah," she answered with her lips quivering.

"Give him a chance. Forgive him. Don't just do it for him, do it for you. You'll feel much better and feel stronger for having tried."

It was as private a conversation as you could have on a plane. We were sitting in the row right by the plane's right propeller, which droned out the possibility of eavesdroppers.

"I think I'm going to do it," she said. "If I didn't want to try I wouldn't have gotten on this plane. Who's picking you up?" she asked me.

"Well, there's an interesting person waiting for me at the airport too. A couple of years ago my mother died from cancer. My father is getting married again. The woman he is marrying is my ride. I met her briefly a couple of years back, but we've never spoken a word to each other. So you're going to meet your new and improved dad, and I'm going to meet my new mom. How about that? We have a lot more in common than you realize."

Nicole's mouth hit the floor when I said it, and within minutes the wheels of the plane hit the runway at TF Green Airport. After the plane pulled up to the gate, we collected our belongings and walked off the plane together. My teenage friend walked right into the arms of a man who had flowers in his hands and tears in his eyes. He looked just like his daughter. It was a wonderful reunion that only three people truly understood the magnitude of—Nicole, her dad and I!

Behind the weeping father and daughter was a smiling woman with short brown hair and an oxford blouse. She had her hands by her side. I walked right up and extended my arms to embrace her.

"Hi, Mary," I said.

I gave her a kiss and off we went to fetch my luggage from the baggage carousel. We chatted the whole way there, and the whole way home to Ledyard in the car. Mary is easy to talk to and has given my dad so much to live for after the death of my mom. Just as we don't choose our parents, the same is true for steps. But I'll tell you, if given the choice, I couldn't have picked anyone better than Mary.

One thing we talked about on the hour ride back to Ledyard was Daisy.

"So, Mary, are you a dog person?" I asked.

"Not really, but your father is," Mary said with a laugh.

BOB

Mary accepted that I needed a dog in my life. She said she just kind of knew it came with the territory. And even if she didn't share my feelings, she very much understood that a dog wasn't just something for me to have, it was a part of who I was. It was that understanding that picked me up from a dark time in my life and that would follow a dark discovery that all dog owners dread.

It was a Sunday morning about two weeks before Christmas 2003. I woke up early. I walked into the kitchen and made myself some Taster's Choice instant coffee. While the water was heating up, I nibbled on a piece of crumb cake. When the microwave oven beeped, I took the mug out and added a scoop of coffee crystals. I followed that with a dash of cream and two scoops of sugar. It was a normal morning.

I walked to the laundry room where Daisy slept. When I opened the door, I couldn't believe what I saw. Daisy was on her back with her legs sort of sticking up in the air. The air went out of my lungs. I stepped back and looked in the direction of the kitchen and den to see if Mary was there. Then I looked back at Daisy to confirm what I thought I knew. I took a slow walk to the den where I found Mary sitting in her chair reading a book.

"She's dead," I told her.

Mary got up very quickly and she was also shocked. Daisy was not a particularly endearing dog, but strangely enough I loved her.

MICHAEL

In the ten years of Daisy's life, a lot happened in mine. I went away to college and later moved to San Francisco. How did I feel when I found out about Daisy? I don't know that I was sad, I guess I was relieved. And as sad as Dad was, I thought he and Mary would eventually be better off without her.

BOB

I went into a deep, deep funk after Daisy died. I was depressed. The holidays were coming, though, and Mary's family would be visiting. Kevin McGrattan and his wife and children would be driving up from Maryland. Kevin asked if he could bring his dog. I said sure. A week and a half later, in came Kevin with his wife, Laura, kids Brian and Susan, and Lizzie, a Corgi. Lizzie was a doll and brought back all my memories, feelings, and ideals about what a dog should be. It was great to have Lizzie with us—and the McGrattans too!

When the McGrattans left and took their dog with them, my funk came back. I knew it, and so did Mary. Mary was so helpful to me in my mourning. Then she said the best thing ever, "Go get yourself a dog."

NINE

A Child's First Dog and First Loss

SAMANTHA WALSH

I am Samantha. I am ten years old. Tiffany was my big sister. She was born before me. We moved from California to Delaware in 2003, when I was a year and a half old. Tiffany came with us and rode in her crate under the airplane.

I love dogs, especially German Shepherds. Right now we have Beverly. She replaced Tiffany. We got Beverly in the fall of 2008 after Tiffany died. Beverly's really cute. She's reddish, tan, and black and has really big ears that look like triangles on her head. She also has black dots on her muzzle that look like freckles. I really love Beverly, but I really miss Tiffany.

Samantha Walsh, Wellesley, Mass., 2010

Samantha Walsh, aka Sammy or Sam, is ten years old. She is the daughter of Kevin and Jean and is Bob's granddaughter. She calls Bob "Grandpops."

She has raised two dogs so far. Her favorite activities include walking her German Shepherd, Beverly, and reading books. Since teaching herself how to read at age three, Samantha has been writing short stories. When the opportunity came to join her dad and grandfather in writing this book, she was ready. When she's not on the computer, she hangs out with her sister, Amanda, enjoying time together at the neighborhood playground. Samantha plans to become a veterinarian.

I remember the day we lost Tiffany when we lived in Wilmington, Delaware. We were not home for several hours. First we went to church at Immaculate Heart of Mary. After church, my father wanted to take us swimming and for a car ride in the country. We swam in the indoor pool at the JCC. We climbed on Daddy's back and did submarines. We take a deep breath, hold onto his shoulders and go for a ride as he swims underwater. That's a submarine.

After we finished swimming, Daddy [Kevin Walsh] drove us by Vice President Biden's house in Greenville, Delaware. Mr. Biden lives right near Tatnall School, which is where my neighbors—Natalie and Stephanie Burrus—went to school when they were teenagers. Natalie and Stephanie are older now. There were a lot of police cars around Mr. Biden's house, but Daddy said nobody was hurt. He says the police follow Vice President Biden around because he's important.

Later Daddy said, "Let's go get water ice!"

My dad loves water ice. He took me, my mother, and my sister to a water ice place near St. Francis Hospital. St. Francis is where my sister, Amanda, was born. Dad got watermelon, Amanda got cherry, Mom got lemon. I wasn't a big fan of water ice, so I told my mom. My mother asked the man in the window if they had any ice cream.

"Sorry, but we don't sell ice cream. We only sell water ice," he told her.

"I will ask your father if he can drive us to McDonald's and get you an M&M McFlurry," Mom said.

Dad drove us to the McDonald's on Wilmington Pike near St. Mary Magdalene's, and across the street from the Charcoal Pit. It's the same McDonald's that bought our blue shirts for our softball team. My dad went inside and ordered me an M&M McFlurry. He doesn't like the drive-thru because he thinks it takes too long. Then we drove home. By the time we got home, I finished my ice cream. We were parked on the driveway for a minute, and then we got out of the car.

Samantha fishing with Tiffany, Brandywine Creek, Wilmington, Del., 2005

Daddy walked up to the front door of the house and unlocked it. Tiffany would always come when Daddy called her name. But Tiffany did not come to the door when Daddy said, "Come, Tiffany!"

It was late in the afternoon, and I came into the house about a minute after Daddy and Mommy did. I saw Daddy leaning on the stair railing holding his head. Mommy was sitting on the steps and she was crying. So I asked, "What's wrong?"

"Hold on a second," Daddy said.

By now Amanda had come inside the side door and was playing in Mom and Dad's room. Daddy called out to her, "Amanda!"

Amanda came running. We did not know what the thing was. We stood right in front of our father facing him. He said, "Listen to me closely. Do you know how Tiffany had a good life?"

We nodded yes.

"Tiffany died while we were gone," he told us.

Our lips shivered and our eyes filled up with tear balls. We followed Daddy into the family room and dead Tiffany was lying on the alphabet rug near the TV. It was too hard for me to say goodbye to her. My heart felt like it was going to rip and create a big hole in it. It also felt like my heart was going to lump up in my throat and break.

So then I did not blurt the words out normally. It was like this, "B ... bye Ti ... if ... ffers."

I looked at Tiffany and she was really still. She was cold like the wind and hard like a turtle. The inside of her ears were white instead of pink. Half of her tongue was sticking out and it was purple and gray, instead of light pink. It was a little shriveled up and twisted.

Then Daddy went over to the Shoemakers' house and rang the doorbell. Mr. Shoe (that's what us kids call him) came back with Daddy. I said, "Mr. Shoe! Mr. Shoe! Tiffany died! She is gone!"

Mr. Shoe said he knew that. I ran outside with Amanda and Mom. Amanda and I were crying. Mommy was too.

Mrs. Burrus was on her driveway across the street. Mrs. Burrus is Gracie's mom. Gracie is my friend. Mrs. Burrus has short blonde hair. Mrs. Burrus came walking down her driveway, looked both ways, and crossed the street. She came onto our driveway. She said, "I am so sorry for the loss of Tiffany."

She patted me and Amanda's heads gently. I said to myself, "How does she know what happened?"

Mrs. Burrus is a very nice and caring lady. Then I ran to the Shoes' backyard and I saw my other friend Zoe Barker walking over. I said, "Tiffany died! Tiffany died!"

Then I went out to the road and I saw Gracie Burrus walking over to our driveway. I ran over to her and shouted, "Tiffany died! Tiffany died!"

Just like her mommy, Gracie said, "I am sorry for the loss of your dog Tiffany."

I accepted that. Gracie looked like she was as sad as me. Then Jackie and Jessie Shoemaker came up the hill and they asked, "What's wrong, Samantha and Amanda?"

I shouted, "Tiffany died! Tiffany died!"

They went back inside their house and they wrote a card for us. It said, "Sorry that your dog died!"

Samantha with Tiffany, Webster Farm, Wilmington, Del., 2006

The card was white with crayon writing on it. I didn't mean to shout at Jackie and Jessie. It just came out that way. I noticed the card they made was very good. I loved the artwork they did. The card was cute-looking and in good shape.

While I was talking with the Shoe girls, Mr. Shoe pulled his brown truck into our driveway. He went into the house with my dad. They came out carrying a picnic blanket. Tiffany's paws were sticking up out of the blanket. They put the blanket and Tiffany in the back of Mr. Shoe's truck. I asked my dad if I could see Tiffany one more time. He said yes. Tiffany was just lying there. By now I could talk better.

"Goodbye, Tiffany," I said.

Mr. Shoe and Daddy got into the truck and drove away. It was the last time I saw my dog.

———

Bob: *"Oh my goodness. Do we really need so many details? I don't know that I want to hear any more sad stories about dogs. I don't know that anyone else does either. I have dogs because they make me happy. I just want to hear happy stories about dogs."*

Kevin: *"Whoa—hold on, Dad. I know what you mean and I get where you're coming from. You're retired and enjoying your golden years. You want only what brings you joy, not sorrow. But don't you see joy and sorrow are inseparable? Leave it to a child, your granddaughter, to remind us of that. Don't worry. Wait until you read what Samantha writes about the joy of bringing a new puppy home.*

"Let me remind you of a book I gave you a few years back. Remember The Prophet? *In Kahlil Gibran's masterpiece, he spoke of pain through the voice of Almustafa, The Chosen and The Beloved. It reads in part:*

> *Your joy is your sorrow unmasked.*

> *And the selfsame well from which your laughter rises was oftentimes filled with your tears.*

> *And how else can it be?*

> *The deeper that sorrow carves into your being, the more joy you can contain.*

> *Some of you say, "Joy is greater than sorrow," and others say, "Nay, sorrow is the greater."*

> *But I say unto you, they are inseparable.*

"I don't think you can fully appreciate how much a dog means until you lose one. It doesn't get any easier each time you go through it. What always gets us through the tough stretch is the joy that we know will come on the day we welcome a new dog into our hearts, and into our homes. We also cherish memories of good times with other departed dogs.

"If you've been raised in a home where dogs have always been the primary pet, you're probably as comfortable with that constancy as your parents are with their collection of forks,

knives, spoons, and cereal bowls. I can still visit my folks, have
a bowl of Rice Krispies, and go back in time forty years. It is the
same with dogs. With dogs, I always know someone is happy
to see me when I come home. They are not just living creatures
inside of my house; they are a part of my lifestyle, a culture.
You gave that culture to me, Dad, and I've passed it on to my
children. For that, I thank you."

Samantha: *"I thank you too, Grandpops. I still think about*
Tiffany a lot and it makes me sad that she's gone. But when I
look over at my new dog Beverly, I start to feel better. Sometimes
I call Beverly over and hug her, while I'm thinking about
Tiffany. I'm just glad we got another dog really soon after
Tiffany died. Beverly makes me really happy."

KEVIN

We had a good run with Tiffany. She gave us twelve
years of love and companionship. Born right around
Christmas in 1996, she had a Golden Retriever's
disposition in a German Shepherd's body. We should
all be so lucky. Tiffany was as pleasing as pie, and that's
not merely opinion. That was fact. Anyone who knew her
would tell you.

Prior to purchasing Tiffany, I lived five dogless years,
and not by choice. In my attempt to become the next Tom
Brokaw, I accepted jobs in television news in two of the

most inhospitable places in the world—for dogs. Oh, there are dogs in the U.S. Territory of Guam, located about a thousand miles southeast of the Philippines. But Guam's dogs are among the most motley and least desirable of dogs you can imagine. There is a serious overpopulation of what the local Chamorro people call "boonie dogs." They are flea-infested strays who rule the streets when the wild chickens go into the brush for a nap.

The sheer number of boonie dogs is unsightly. It isn't uncommon to see a dog sleeping right at the foot of your car door. A nudge with your foot might cost you a toe, or produce nothing at all. If the goal is to get into your car, you might have to use the side door. Then you'll have to be careful backing out, because the dog probably won't move.

One time in 1994, while driving through the Village of Tamuning on East Agana Bay, I turned a corner in my little Toyota Tercel only to see a large boonie dog asleep in the middle of the street. There wasn't enough room to get by without having to drive off the pavement. With the 200-yard gap closing, I saw the dog's left ear lift up from its still body. It rotated in the direction of my car as if it were calculating my distance away by sound waves.

I slowed to about 10 miles per hour and coasted with my foot resting gently on the brake. The dog slowly lifted its hindquarters and slid its hind legs underneath him. I knew it was a male because I could see the appropriate undercarriage. He moved with the motivation of a drunk awakened from a deep slumber.

At glacial speed he raised his torso, pulling his front legs in. That put him on all fours, but without the balance you might expect from having all posts planted. He did a slow spine and hamstring stretch with a few wobbles. Moving left instead of right, he turned his head and body around without ever looking back in the direction of my car. By the time I reached the potential impact zone, he was out of the way by the wisp of a hair on his flea-bitten tail. I sensed the dog had probably done this hundreds of times before.

No sooner had I passed, I looked in the rearview mirror and saw the dog saunter back to the same spot. He plopped right back down in the middle of the road. He was not about to let neighborhood traffic interfere with his place of rest.

We lived in a condo that didn't allow dogs as pets. But even if we lived in a house and wanted a new friend, taking in a boonie dog from the wild was out of the question. Local shelters didn't offer much more. That left bringing in a dog from the mainland—which really was a whole other kettle of Manahac (Chamorro for rabbit fish).

Guam is rabies free. The only way the disease could get a footing on the island was if a rabid animal brought it in from the outside. Island law requires all dogs coming into the territory to be quarantined at owner's expense for six months. Families who moved to Guam, including the U.S. military, were thousands of dollars poorer for it in the end. Many of the dogs came out of quarantine in poor health. The separation anxiety for all involved was almost unbearable.

When we moved to Hawaii in 1995, after the two-year Guam television tour, we started thinking about buying a dog. We found out the state had the same quarantine process as Guam. So, sadly for us, it was another two years sans dog.

By the time we moved back to the mainland in 1997, to start a six-year tour in Fresno, California, finding a dog was as important to me as finding a house was to my wife, Jean. Jean had a small Yorkshire Terrier named Fluffy growing up, so the concept of having a dog wasn't completely foreign to her. What she didn't expect, and fully embrace from the start, was my choice of breed. I wanted to go big, and I really wanted a German Shepherd.

"Do we have to have something that big?" Jean asked.

"Yes," I told her, "I've had small dogs and big ones. I just think with me anchoring the evening news and not coming home until very late at night, you might want a big dog for protection and peace of mind. There's nothing better for that than a German Shepherd."

To that Jean was receptive. We started looking in *The Fresno Bee* and eventually found a female German Shepherd for the very low price of $75. We went to see the dog that was living in a small apartment in the city. The dog's owner was a nice young man named Tony, who later became a Madera County Sheriff's Deputy. Tony was heartbroken that he would have to let his adorable ten-week-old puppy go, but with his future wife expecting their first child, he knew the dog needed a bigger home.

The puppy he called Nikko greeted us with licks, nips, and rancid puppy breath. She was more blonde than tan, with a black muzzle and the usual German Shepherd moles and markings. Her ears were enormous, and only able to stand up halfway. She was a bundle of energy who expressed love easily. We knew it wouldn't be easy raising a dog that would need a lot of attention and care, but I didn't care. I made an offer on the spot.

"We really like the dog and want to take her. However, we don't move into our home until the end of the month. If I pay you a little bit more, would you keep her another couple of weeks?" I asked Tony.

"Sure," Tony said, relieved to have a buyer, but also happy that he had a good excuse to hold onto the dog a little while longer.

So I gave Tony $100 cash. In essence, we bought our first dog as a couple before we bought our first house.

On the ride home, Jean and I talked about renaming Nikko. I liked the name Tiffany.

"Do you think she'll be confused about the name change?" Jean asked.

"Nah, she's too young. She only knows what we say. She probably doesn't even know her name right now."

Three weeks later it was time to bring Tiffany home. She would move into our first house on Seacrest Drive only a day after we did. There were so many new things going on in our life and I was really excited. Jean was a bit anxious though. She never really immersed herself in the raising of her childhood dog, but now she was about to become a primary caretaker and momma figure.

The day of Tiffany's big homecoming turned out to be a big day on TV too. I was unable to get away from breaking news coverage at our TV station, so Jean had to trek into the city by herself to pick up the dog.

"I tried to put Tiffany in the backseat of the car, and she would have no part of it," Jean says. "She jumped up into the front seat and onto my lap. She kept crying and trying to climb up my chest to lick my face. Her claws were sharp and so were her teeth. In trying to keep her away from my face so I could keep my eye on the road, I had to slow down. I drove about 15 miles per hour and had to pull over constantly. It took 15 minutes to get there, but it took about an hour to get home."

Once they got home, Jean took Tiffany for a walk around the backyard hoping she would pee. No luck. The minute they got inside the house, though, Tiffany squatted and wet the living room rug. Within an hour, she did the same thing at the top of the stairs. Tiffany was leaving her mark in more ways and places than one, and doing so quickly. There would be a few more accidents before the night was done.

By the time I got home from work, Jean was exhausted and asleep on the couch. I came into the house through the garage and was the recipient of a flying tackle and a front paw to a most sensitive place. Hello, Tiffany! I bent over more from reaction than from pain. Tiffany tilted her head to the left, the right, and then invaded my personal space once more to lick my face. I patted her head and said, "Oh, Tiffany, I'm so happy to see you."

She felt the same and celebrated by leaving a puddle in front of my shoes. In Tiffany, I was hoping to have a good friend who knew she had a job to do by guarding the house while I was away or asleep upstairs. That meant I wanted her to sleep on the ground floor of the house. But keeping her downstairs uncrated wasn't going to be easy. Tiffany wanted to be everywhere we were. That first night I blocked the stairs with no fewer than a dozen cardboard boxes stacked tightly between the banister and the wall. The boxes were tall enough that a leap over them seemed unlikely.

Over the next half hour we were serenaded by a cacophony of whines, wails, and barking. It was hard to tell who was suffering more—us or Tiffany.

"Do you think she's okay?" Jean asked as we faced one another with heads on our pillows.

"She's fine. She's just fussing. She'll eventually tire herself out and fall asleep. I want her to know that she sleeps downstairs and that it's her job to guard the house. If she comes up here, she might get too comfortable and lose focus. I don't want her up here snuggling in bed. In fact, I don't want her in our bed at all. I want her working down there. Don't give in. It will only reward her. We have to toughen up."

As soon as I said that, we heard boxes tumbling down, followed by the familiar jingling of dog chains. They got louder as Tiffany got closer. Pretty soon we felt the impact of Tiffany landing on our bed. Hello, Tiffany, once more!

Fortunately she didn't wet the bed, but she left us wet with licks to the face.

Jean found it cute, but I was determined to get Tiffany back on patrol. I scooped her up under my arm and brought her back downstairs. She knew what was up and tried to wriggle away. I squeezed her closer to my side as she whimpered and nipped at my fingers. I told her to stop. She only fought harder.

When I got to the ground floor, I put her down and started to reach for one of the scattered boxes. I grabbed a box and turned in the direction of the stairs to replace it on the stack. In the course of the turning motion, she leaped through the hole in the boxes and went bounding back up the stairs.

"Aaah! Hi, Tiffany!" I could hear Jean's voice, followed by laughter.

I ran back upstairs to retrieve the dog only to find her snuggled against my wife's chest and Jean giving her kisses on the top of her head.

"Oh isn't she cute?" Jean asked.

Tiffany gave me a sad look with convincing eyes and heart-breaking head tilts. I didn't want to fall for it.

"Gimme the dog," I said semi-firmly while holding back a laugh.

"Oh, can't we just let her spend the night up here with us?" Jean asked. "It's her first night and obviously she's scared."

"Hey look, it's gonna be rough for a while, but she'll get used to it and eventually she'll thrive on the responsibility of having a job," I told her.

So I lifted Tiffany up and back down the stairs we went. This time I put her inside the crate while I reassembled the barrier of boxes. I even stuck a few bath towels between the boxes to tighten the fit. Feeling as though Tiffany would not be able to wedge her way through, I climbed along the narrow shelf of steps outside the banister and swung my right leg over the railing, leaving me sitting atop the rail in a horse-riding position. With a little lean to the right and a hop, I lifted my left leg over and onto the stairs.

Before heading up, I looked back to see Tiffany sporting a tear-your-heart-out, woe-is-me look on her cute puppy face. I looked back at her, crinkled my face sympathetically and said, "I know it's hard, Tiffany, but you have to be brave. Stay down here and guard the house."

Not able to take it any longer, I headed up the stairs and into the bedroom. I lifted the covers of the comforter and slid into bed where Jean waited anxiously for an update on the dog.

"Are you sure she's okay?" Jean asked.

"She'll have to be. We'll see how long that lasts."

After a few minutes of small talk, we once again heard the tumbling sound of boxes followed by the jingling sound of Tiffany's chain and tags. Within seconds, the master escape artist was rocketing onto our bed with a happy and hopeful look that we would cave in, which we did finally. I didn't feel good about it; I was simply too tired to fight the good fight on this night.

Tiffany just wouldn't be denied. There was no keeping her away from us. I figured if she was this determined to be so close to us, she'd more than take care of business if anyone attempted to harm us. Her quickly emerging love for us, and desire to be nearby at all times, was overwhelming and touching. As we settled in for the night, Jean caressed the dog instead of me. It was beautiful to watch, and I felt very lucky to have Tiffany immersed in our lives.

Of course, Tiffany gave us plenty of reasons to be frustrated with the joy of raising a puppy. The housebreaking took a month or so, which meant lots of cleaning up. The greatest damage was to shoes and furniture, as Tiffany sought to take out the pain of her teething on anything chewable. Jean and I joked that Tiffany was cheap in terms of how much she cost when we bought her, but when you added up the damages, she cost us a small fortune! Even when we caught her acting mischievously, she was impossible not to love because she wilted at even the slightest raising of the voice or show of displeasure.

When we finally had Tiffany housebroken, I installed a doggie door so she could let herself out of the house to relieve herself when she wished. Jean took her to obedience classes, and Tiffany started to take commands more readily. Jean taught me what she and Tiffany learned in class, and I practiced with Tiffany at home. Within a few months, she had the commands down cold and would take them from just about anyone. It made her a joy to all who loved to see a dog with discipline.

Disciplined dogs always get a lot of attention. I think it's because people have a fascination with trained animals. For the most part, much of that witness is limited to what we see in films and on TV. To see a well-trained dog in person is impressive. I would take Tiffany to Woodward Park to practice her obedience training. People took notice.

"Tiffany, sit. Good girl. Tiffany, lie down. Good girl. Tiffany, fetch. Good girl."

"How do you get her to do that?" they would ask as if there was some sort of magic.

"It's just repetition and praise," I told them. "You do the same command over and over and praise her when she's done. I used to give her treats. Now praise is reward enough."

Obedience is one thing, tricks are another. I define a trick as anything that looks really cool. Tiffany would fetch anything. But nothing—and I mean nothing—attracted more people's attention than Tiffany fetching golf balls.

The fact that Tiffany loved to fetch golf balls served more than one purpose: it was great fun and exercise for her, and for me it was a chance to brush up on my short game. I have no doubt Tiffany helped me shave a few strokes off my score.

Our swimming pool in the backyard only added to the fun. To create a real golf course scenario, I treated the pool as a greenside bunker with a pin tucked tightly behind on the green. To get the ball close to the hole, I had to play a 30 foot flop shot that would land just over the hazard's edge, but not more than a foot or two past. That meant landing the ball on the narrow, pebbled collar that circled the outside of the pool. It was the touchiest of touch shots. If I didn't hit it hard enough, the ball would end up in the drink. If I hit it too hard, it would land on the grass beyond the pool's collar.

Coming up short was always the harder end of the deal. I'd have to jump into the pool to retrieve the ball, which at the very least involved disrobing. Tiffany would have no part of taking the plunge. In the spring, summer, and fall an impromptu swim was no problem. Winter?

Big problem. Daytime winter temperatures in Central California are often in the forties. That'll put a chill in your body that can only be cured by getting wet once more. A long, hot shower will do the trick, but set you back about a half hour. Eventually, I smartened up and fished the balls out with a skimmer. All the while, Tiffany would bark at me for the interruption in play.

Back and forth Tiffany would run. She'd sit off to the side as I rolled a Titleist Pro V1 ball up onto a tuft of grass, and she would wait until I struck the ball. At impact she'd take off with such force that she'd send divots flying backward. When she got onto the pebbled walkway, you could hear her long nails scratching the surface while digging in for traction. If I hit the flop shot just right, it would bounce on the narrow collar and Tiffany would launch herself airborne to catch it before it hit the ground again on the grass.

Sometimes I hit it too hard—forcing Tiffany to do a smother tackle to keep the ball from continuing on into the flower beds. I didn't want that to happen because the flowers usually came out on the short end of a trampling. The pressure to perform in the backyard and to avoid fishing in the pool or an expensive trip to the nursery was good training for Friday morning golf games with my pals. I never stressed about short-siding myself with tough pin placements. I had already pulled off those delicate shots plenty of times before with Tiffany.

When the grass needed time to heal in the backyard, we'd switch to the front. That of course brought more viewers. Be it in the form of walkers, or people driving their cars slowly around the corner of Lighthouse and Seacrest Drives, plenty of people stopped to watch Tiffany play.

"How did you teach her to do that?" more than a few would ask.

"I just hit it and she goes and gets it."

"Does she ever swallow the golf balls?"

"Not yet."

"Isn't that bad for her teeth?"

"No worse than a bone."

"That is the coolest thing I've ever seen!"

When we'd take Tiffany for a walk, we were often recognized because of her, and not so much for us: "Hey, isn't that the dog that fetches golf balls?"

"Yes it is," we'd tell them.

It wasn't just golf balls. Tiffany would fetch anything for anyone—balls, Frisbees, etc.

Children in the neighborhood would knock on the front door of our house and ask for Tiffany. "Is this where the German Shepherd lives?" they'd ask as Tiffany would peer out from between our legs.

"Yes, it is."

"Well, can we take her for a walk?"

With that, we'd grab the leash and hand the dog over. She'd be gone for a half hour or so, and she always came back happy. Tiffany would walk and hang out with anybody.

Even when we were at church, work, or out running errands, neighbors would walk her on their own. The Lorbers who lived across the street had their own leash for Tiffany. I can't tell you how many times I'd be pulling into the neighborhood and see my dog being walked by two happy adults, Kevin and Elizabeth Lorber. They'd look over our back fence, call Tiffany's name, and open the side gate for her. Off they'd go. It was great. We had a rotation of walkers.

Sometimes Tiffany would just go over to the Lorbers or the Crossmans and plunk herself down on either family's front lawn. She'd watch them toil in the garden. Tiffany could've been a pink flamingo.

Tiffany even did security checks and overnighters. We got a call one night from Elizabeth Lorber, "I heard a sound in the house. Could you bring Tiffany over and have a look?"

"C'mon, Tiff. We got a job to do," I said as I grabbed her leash.

From the tone of my voice Tiffany realized this was more than just a friendly visit. Her body language was different, and she was aggressively pulling as we crossed the street. She hardly even acknowledged Elizabeth when we entered the house.

"Somebody here, Tiff? Sniff around, find him."

I didn't need to do anything else. Tiffany instinctively knew to sniff around under beds, couches, in the closets, and anywhere else a person could hide. She was a natural—despite no training. With the coast clear Elizabeth asked if Tiffany could spend the night as her husband, Kevin, was away on business. Tiffany was more than happy to be a snuggle partner.

Tiffany became a regular house guest at the Lorbers, based on Kevin Lorber's travel schedule. Kevin would leave town, Elizabeth would call, and Tiffany would be out the door and on her way over. The Lorbers' house was Tiffany's home away from home. It was good for Elizabeth, and it was good for us to have Tiffany out of our house for a bit. With her gone, we could rake the carpets from her heavy shedding.

The Lorbers loved Tiffany so much that for a time they considered getting a dog too. That's really saying something because Kevin Lorber was allergic to dogs. Tiffany's visits would sometimes cause him to have bouts of sneezing and watery eyes, but he put up with it because it was worth it.

Aside from love and protection, Tiffany brought something else to the neighborhood that transcended anything I thought a dog could do. One day—when I was throwing Tiffany the Frisbee on the front lawn—two pairs of sisters came over to join us. There was squabbling among the four girls over who would get to throw the Frisbee next. The older girls tried to squeeze the younger ones out. As I was trying to referee the difficult moment, Tiffany solved the problem. After each subsequent throw she'd bring the Frisbee back to a different child an equal number of times. It was clear she understood the concept of sharing.

How did this happen? I don't know. I never showed her how to do it. I'm not even sure I could if I tried. Tiffany completely defused the situation. The children's parents noticed it too.

"That is one special dog," Ann Crossman said.

In 2003, life and career opportunities took us back East where we settled in Wilmington, Delaware. Part of the Philadelphia metropolitan area and about thirty miles south of Center City, Wilmington, in the minds of many, is the best-kept secret in the region. There's no sales tax in Delaware. Home prices and property taxes are a fraction of what they are in Pennsylvania and New Jersey. The quality of life is rich, without the necessary riches.

Jean and Kevin Walsh, Wilmington, Del., 2007

Wilmington's central location is perfect for commuting. It is about thirty minutes to Philadelphia by car or rail. New York and Washington are about two-hour drives away, and even less if you take Amtrak. I know plenty of people who live in Wilmington and take the train to D.C. or Manhattan daily. You could go to the Wilmington train station every morning at 6:30 and see Delaware's Congressional delegation waiting for the Acela to take them to Washington.

Vice President Joe Biden was then a senator, and very approachable. He moved easily among the early morning commuters, chatting with them and sharing laughs. The same was true with former Congressman Mike Castle and Senator Tom Carper. They didn't have quite the schmooze factor that Senator Biden did, but, then again, few do.

Wilmington has a lot of charm. It's a self-sufficient city with plenty of colonial history and architecture to go with a good eating and social scene. You can get a stellar meal, with wine, for about half what you'd pay in bigger cities. No sales tax and free parking go a long way too. If you wanted more, you could always upgrade by going to Philly, New York, or D.C.

In looking for a house, we wanted a place with a pleasing look and a homey feel. We wanted a neighborhood similar to what we had had in California. It would be tough to find that aesthetically, but we knew we could find it in spirit. Webster Farm was that place. Residents spent time outdoors and with each other. It seemed as if everyone had a dog.

Located about six miles north of downtown Wilmington, and about a mile away from I-95, Webster Farm is home to a hundred twenty houses on about thirty acres. The homes are stylish in look, and most are about fifty to sixty years old. The properties are well-kept with most of the folks taking care of their own lawns and gardens. Few are above sweat equity. That serves a couple of purposes. It makes the neighborhood look great and it gives neighbors a communal activity. People chat across their lawns, borrow tools, and share beverages and snacks. They know each other and care about each other.

Taking good care of your property and maintaining curb appeal is an unwritten rule in Webster Farm. The pressure is pervasive. You understand what is expected of you as a homeowner. Unfortunately, the red brick Cape Cod on the one hundred block of Marcella Road was one of those places where the previous homeowner hadn't maintained the standard. A bitter divorce and financial issues left the property overgrown and unsightly. When Jean saw it, she said, "That's the place for us!"

"Really?" I asked. "Are you sure?"

"Yes!" she said. "Don't worry about all the scruffiness. We can clean that up and redo the landscaping. It's a good house and a great neighborhood. It just needs more color and lot of TLC."

We put in an offer and it was accepted. Almost immediately we had the poison ivy and invasive vines removed. We redid the gardens, pulling out the pachysandra and replacing it with new shrubs, Japanese maples, and hostas. We took the old white window shutters off and replaced them with antique blue ones. We painted the front door to match the shutters and fixed the front porch posts. It gave the house a truly new look.

Our arrival in the neighborhood was certainly noticed—not so much for us but for the house makeover and for Tiffany. The front lawn was about 100 feet wide, which gave plenty of room to chip golf balls to Tiffany. She would gobble them up and bring them back.

"That dog is amazing," a neighbor from Jan Drive said as he pulled over to chat, "and the house looks really good. Welcome to the neighborhood."

Tiffany made for easy conversation, which is another good thing about dogs. Dogs do more than connect families; they bring other people, including neighbors, closer together too. I'm sure nobody in Webster Farm had ever seen such a thing as a canine golf ball retriever. And when they met Tiffany and witnessed her gentleness and warmth, they realized she'd be as welcome an addition to the neighborhood as her owners.

Tiffany had a social life all her own in the new neighborhood. Next door, there was a chocolate Labrador Retriever named Amber. Amber was a wonderful dog who welcomed Tiffany heartily. It didn't matter that Amber was the protector of toddler twin sisters. She knew Tiffany was a good soul and a fellow guardian. Tiffany and Amber would play chase together and rest together. And when my children played with the Shoemaker twins, the dogs would guard either end of the Shoemaker property.

On the other side of our house lived the Collins family. They lost their dog not long before we moved into the neighborhood, and they welcomed Tiffany anytime she'd wander over for a visit. Corinne Collins would pull into the driveway in her Honda Pilot, and Tiffany would greet her as she opened the driver-side door.

"Hello, Tiffany!" I'd hear from Corinne as she climbed out of the car. Tiffany would linger for just a few seconds, soaking up affectionate pats on the head, before she would come trotting back to resume whatever it was we were doing on the front lawn.

When we would go away on vacation, Erin and Blaine Collins, then in high school, would take care of Tiffany for us. They had keys to our house and would come over to feed her and take her out so she could do her business. Later, they figured it was easier to have her stay with them at their home. That was fine with us and certainly okay with Tiffany.

Next to the Collinses' house were the Simons. Barb and Gary had a dog named Griffey. Griffey was an English Springer Spaniel from Pennsylvania Dutch Country. Barb and Gary found him on an Amish farm. He was living inside a barn. They brought him home to Delaware. Griffey was a lively male who loved to chase squirrels up trees. Tiffany enjoyed her visits with Griffey, but especially with Barb and Gary. They would pet her and give her treats.

Unlike California, there were no backyard fences in Webster Farm. So the backyards of our homes created a continuous greenway. It was our own private dog park. Back and forth the dogs would run while the dog owners would chat and enjoy the outdoors. The dogs, and their potty needs, gave us a reason to leave the house and venture out back at least five or six times a day. So it was really the dogs that were the vehicle that drove the neighborhood dynamic.

As much as Tiffany was a warm fuzzy to anyone who met her, it took her a while to warm up to our children. I think much of it had to do with jealously. She was our first daughter. When Samantha was born in 2001, we brought her directly to Tiffany for an introduction and inspection. Tiffany took a look and a sniff of Sam's face and then promptly walked away. Tiffany's indifference was a little disappointing because I thought she'd embrace the big sister/friend/guardian role. My guess is Tiffany thought of Sam as a visitor who would eventually leave.

In 2003, we brought home a new baby, Amanda. Like the homecoming of Samantha, we brought Amanda directly to Tiffany for a greeting. The reception this time was different. It had nothing to do with the child, but a deeper recognition of "So, this is what humans do. They have babies and bring babies home."

Suddenly, Tiffany "got it." She warmed up to both kids and made up for lost time.

Tiffany grew to love Sammy and Amanda immensely. She played with them, watched over them, and slept on the floor next to their beds. However, she never liked it when they stuck their faces in hers. "Grrrrrr" I'd hear from time to time.

"Girls, she doesn't like that," I would warn.

We never worried that Tiffany would snap at the children. The low growl was just her way of letting them know she didn't like Eskimo kisses. It was a good lesson for Sam and Amanda about approaching other dogs—especially those they didn't know. It's better to be safe than sorry.

Tiffany provided so many other lessons by simply being herself. Her exemplary obedience set a good example for how others should honor authority. It was easy to say, "If a dog can understand what it is I'm telling her to do, you should have no trouble either."

My children had no comeback for that. With Tiffany, they learned life's lessons in caretaking. They would take turns feeding her and replenishing her water bowl. When the kids would forget, it was another teachable moment about responsibility and accountability.

Amanda and Samantha with Tiffany, Wilmington, Del., 2008

"Amanda, did you forget to feed Tiffany?"

"Yes," she'd answer.

"How would you like it if Mommy and Daddy forgot to feed you?"

"I'd feel bad."

"Well at least you can talk. Tiffany can't. She's probably been hungry for hours. How do you think she feels?"

"She's probably sad and really hungry."

"That's right. That's why you have to always remember to feed her and do it on time. She's counting on you. Don't let her down."

"Okay, Daddy. I'm sorry."

Once the children understood their roles as caretakers, they embraced it. Tiffany became a gracious follower. She rewarded them with appreciation and affection. When Tiffany left us that Sunday afternoon, we lost not only an important member of the family, but also a purpose for taking care of something and someone other than ourselves. We didn't want that feeling to last long. In fact, before the day was done, we started a preliminary search online for Tiffany's replacement.

TEN

Smile, It's Annie

BOB

The fact that Mary told me, in 2004, to get another dog was a powerful acknowledgment. It was further validation of her love for me and all that I am after nine wonderful years of marriage. I need dogs in my life. I am not the same without them. Mary would be just fine without a dog. A dog in the house gets her juices flowing about as much as a goldfish in a bowl, only with a lot more care and supervision needed. But that's not the point. The point is Mary's willing to put up with all of that because she loves me.

After Mary green-lighted me to "go get yourself a dog," I started my search. The first place I looked for a new dog was on the computer. I sat down in my office adjacent to the master bedroom and logged on. As the monitor started flickering with light and life, and the computer accelerated with its familiar whir sound, I caught a good buzz on a natural high and stronger-than-usual morning coffee. I was really jazzed to start a new life journey. Just as the home page for MSN popped up, I was starting to feel like my old self again.

Naturally I went right to Google. I typed in Cairn Terriers. Cairns have been so good to me in the past, so I figured why not go with what you know. But I couldn't get the McGrattan's little Corgi, Lizzie, out of my mind. She was such a good dog and I liked everything about her. She loved without gushing. Her look, disposition, size, and spirit were perfect. She was everything that Daisy the Dalmatian wasn't.

Before I knew it, a few hours of my Internet search had passed. Eventually, Mary came calling.

"Bob, lunch is ready. Take a break and have something to eat," she said.

Over lunch I told her about my search. I was thrilled. She was happy that I was happy. I shared with her just about everything I'd found online that morning. I couldn't believe how much information could be found in so little time. Had I done it "the old way," I think it would have taken me about six months to research what I'd accomplished in just a couple of hours. I felt good about the work and what it would lead to for me and, God willing, for Mary.

"Well how soon do you think you might be looking to make a purchase?" Mary asked.

"Oh, as soon as I can," I told her, "but I want to make sure I get it right in terms of breed, personality, and everything else."

"What did you think about Lizzie when she was here for the holidays?" Mary asked.

"She was lovely, just lovely. I loved everything about her."

"Well why don't you call Kevin [Kevin McGrattan is Mary's son] and see if he can give you the number of Lizzie's breeder."

Great idea. I thought about that too, and Mary—once again—provided a gentle push that made it easier to follow my plan and my heart. I went over to the refrigerator where a long list of family telephone numbers and addresses is stuck to the side with a magnet. The front of the fridge is littered with pictures of all the kids, grandkids, and family dogs over the years.

"It's a memorial to dead dogs," Mary jokes.

That's mostly true, but not completely true. There are a few living ones up there, and I was looking forward to adding another picture of a puppy to the collage. So I called Kevin McGrattan's wife, Laura, and got the number of their breeder.

Bob's wife Mary refers to the refrigerator in their house
as a "memorial to dead dogs."

I was glowing when I dialed the breeder in Maryland
because I was so hopeful about the future. This was the
next step and a big one. But whatever positivity I had
disappeared, almost as soon as the conversation started.

The breeder was clearly distraught. She had a recent
litter of Corgis and lost them all. This was totally
inexplicable to the woman who seemed to be on the verge
of tears. She explained that she had been breeding Corgis
for years and that this was the first time she had lost every

one of the pups in a litter. I certainly commiserated with her on her loss.

I asked her if she could recommend other reputable breeders. She directed me to one in Landenberg, Pennsylvania. I called that breeder, and she indicated that she had a small female that was born in October. She was wondering if I'd like to come see her. Would I like to? Oh, absolutely I'd like to.

Landenberg is about a forty-five-minute drive from where Kevin and Jean were living then in Wilmington, Delaware. The next morning, Mary and I packed the car and drove from Connecticut to Delaware. We would spend the night at Kevin's house and visit the breeder the next day.

When we arrived at Kevin's home on Marcella Road, Jean welcomed us in. So did their German Shepherd Tiffany. Tiffany was in her golden years: grayer and slower, but still a jewel in how she carried herself and treated others. She was interested in everyone and everything. She was never overbearing in any way. She was special.

Kevin came home later in the day, and we talked over dinner about visiting the breeder. After the meal, the ladies and the young grandkids retired to the den next to the kitchen for playtime. Kevin and I went to his office upstairs. Tiffany followed us. We talked about dogs and life and how to find the breeder's home in Landenberg. Kevin printed out directions on MapQuest.

Before too long it was time to settle in for the night. Mary joined me in the upstairs guest bedroom, and Tiffany slept on the floor.

We awoke the next morning with great anticipation. Kevin was up and out early, getting in a morning workout before appearing on TV. We watched him on the old Your Morning news program on the CN8 Network. He's a pro and he's funny when appropriate. I don't know where his inner performer comes from, certainly not from me. It's fun to watch your son on TV. Not many fathers get the chance.

Jean made us eggs Benedict and coffee for breakfast. It was delightful. At around 9:30 Jean gave us cups of coffee to go, and we were off to the breeder. The plan was to go there, see the dog, maybe buy it—that was my hope— return to Kevin's, and spend another night. The drive to Landenberg was pleasant and not too long. We drove through the rolling hills of Chester County where farming and open space are still ways of life.

Just like the MapQuest directions indicated, we found ourselves turning into the breeder's driveway after about forty-five minutes on the road.

The kennel was located on a hillside with a long approach up a winding driveway. The grounds were nicely trimmed, and a dog obedience training ground was set up on the lawn. There were ramps, posts, jumps—all those obstacles you see on The Animal Channel.

We rang the bell and the breeder came to the door, without a pup. We chit chatted for a little while and I guess she found us to be okay. She asked if we'd like to see the little puppy we had talked about. "Yes, oh yes," I told her.

Annie (yes, she smiles)

She absented herself for what seemed like a very long time, at least four or five minutes. She came back to the kitchen with the cutest little pup in her arms.

Unlike Kevin McGrattan's Corgi, which had tinges of black in addition to tan and white, this one was all tan and white, with stellar markings. I gulped as the breeder put the puppy down on the floor and the dog ran to me, then to Mary, then back to me with a smile on her saucy little face. That dog had a smile on her face! She kissed us both, several times.

As soon as I saw her, I knew we had a puppy. So did Mary. It wasn't just something you thought, it was something you felt. Mary knew my misery was over. I think that the joy of the moment may have persuaded her to start thinking of dogs as more than a pet—rather, a way of life, just like I did. My father shared the gift of raising dogs with me, I shared it with my sons, and now my children have shared it with their children.

We paid the asking price and asked the breeder if she had a spare leash and collar. She did. We went to a local pet supply house, purchased a small crate and sundry items and returned to pick up our special pup that we would name Annie. Already she had become a new member of my clan.

We brought her back to Kevin's house, and I couldn't have been more proud. I was one very happy man. When we entered Kevin's house, Tiffany took one look at my new friend and charged. With teeth bared and paws slipping on the hardwood floors, Tiffany put the fear of God in Annie.

Tiffany was a lovable animal, but she was not about to share her home with another dog. So we kept Annie in the crate, and Tiffany gave Annie the *maloik*—Italian slang for "evil eye"—all night long.

Amanda and Samantha with Annie, 2011

After spending the night, we drove home to Connecticut. The pup traveled well, with much attention showered on her. After a stop or two, we pulled into the driveway and Annie was home at last. She sniffed the whole house before settling down.

She's still with us and still smiling eight years later. She loves everyone she meets. She's walked three times a day and cherishes all her fans in the neighborhood that we meet along the way: Miss Ann with Bella, a Golden

Retriever, or Elizabeth and her two small pups in tow. They all know Annie and love her.

Annie's walks begin with me asking her, "Do you want to go for a walk?" She tilts her head and rushes to the door. I give her a Cheerio (just one, mind you), slip on her leash, and off we go. She almost prances when we take our walk. "Do your business," I tell her. She does.

Annie's favorite spot under the kitchen table

I love to fish and Annie loves to follow. I often bring her along to the spots. She knows my fly fishing pals: Al, Doc, Gordon, Frank, Tony, Jay, and Ernie. Yup, all my cronies know Annie and they often give her a treat or two. She smiles contentedly when they stroke her head and she gives them kisses.

When Annie's at home, she sits between Mary and me, wherever we are. She changes her position when we move. She's at our feet when we watch TV. She sits between us while we're eating. When Mary's cooking and I'm in my office at the computer, she splits the difference and hangs out in our den. She's always looking at us with her big blackish/brown eyes. I truly think she's in love with us and the entire world. We love her back.

I think one of the reasons I love Annie so much is that she may be the last dog I'll ever have. It's hard to discuss your own mortality, but let's be honest: when we reach a certain age, we all think about it. I've outlived my brothers and a lot of my friends. Longevity is hardly a hallmark of our family. I think a big part of why I've enjoyed pretty good health into my seventies is that I love my life.

I've been really blessed over the years, and dogs have been such a big part of that. Some dogs were harder to love than others. Let me tell you—Frisky, Fly Boy, and Daisy were no beds of roses. Were it not for them and their thorns, I might not have appreciated how good the other dogs really were. Owning a dog is different from being a parent. You can play favorites. It really did take this long to find mine in Annie. I guess you could say I really did save the best for last.

ELEVEN

Beverly,
A Dog to Lead Us Home

KEVIN

After Tiffany died in 2008, we started looking for a new dog right away. It was good therapy, or so I thought. My wife, Jean, did most of the research online and recruited Samantha to join the effort.

On an early Saturday night, when most young parents had either turned the kids over to a babysitter so they could go out, or rented a movie for the family to watch together, Samantha and I sat down at the computer. Sammy took control of the mouse. Looking over her shoulder, I was heartsick when I saw how much the price of dogs had gone up over the years.

Thirteen years before, we had purchased Tiffany for $100, after responding to an ad in the newspaper. Time and technology changed all that. We didn't even bother with the newspaper this time. The Internet was our new

Kevin and Samantha discussing a new family dog

dog finder, and I found out fast that we might not be able to swing it.

It was not a good time for us financially. I was working for a television network that was undergoing massive restructuring. The future didn't look rosy, so I had to be smart with our money. I turned my head and looked over Samantha's shoulders and into her eyes. She was transfixed on the computer screen and hardly noticed me. She was glowing. The reflection of dogs jumped off the computer screen and danced in her eyes. It was a shining moment and a heartbreaking one at the same time. I just didn't think we could afford a new dog, but I didn't have the heart to tell her.

SAMANTHA

I was still sad because I thought that Tiffany would be mad or upset with us for getting a new dog. I thought that she would think that we did not love her anymore. My dad said, "Don't worry. Tiffany knows we still love her. She'd probably want us to have another dog so we're not so sad anymore."

Mommy and Daddy were talking about maybe having a Golden Retriever, or a boy dog. I would have liked to have had a boy dog. I liked girl dogs as much as boy dogs, but I was really tired of having so many girls in my family. I thought maybe we should get a boy dog because my dad is the only boy in our house. Maybe my dad could have a new pal with him.

KEVIN

I was thinking about a boy dog too. I thought it would be cool to have a German Shepherd named Sarge or Dudley. It just sounds cool doesn't it? I've never had a male dog. The only dogs I've known in my life have all been female. Nothing wrong with that; I just thought I'd like to switch it up. Plus, with two daughters and a wife, that's a lot of girl power in the house. It can be overwhelming.

Also overwhelming was the financial consideration. I still didn't know how I was going to pay for a dog, with most prices ranging from $500 to $4,500. Seeing that there were a lot of dogs available, I thought breeders might be willing to negotiate. I sent a fishing email in the form of a question and offer to a German Shepherd breeder in Chester County, Pennsylvania. "Hello, we live in Delaware. I'm looking at your litter online and the puppies are adorable. However, they are just out beyond our budget at this time. Would you consider selling a puppy for $350?"

It was a shot in the dark, but the number really was about the maximum I could pay at the time. The negative reply came with a cautious tone. "I would be very careful about trying to get a German Shepherd on the cheap. No reputable breeder will sell for less than $1,000. If they do, they're probably a backyard breeder, or a puppy mill."

It was another reality check that sunk my spirits deeper, but the breeder's advice was spot on. The kids were putting me on the spot about making a move on a dog fast. I was torn. I needed a dog as much as they did. Life just wasn't the same without one. But as most people can appreciate, sometimes life and life's reality—financial and otherwise—introduce painful impositions.

On a warm, spectacular late September Sunday afternoon, I visited Brandywine Country Club for some golf therapy. As I started to change from my church clothes into my golf wear in front of locker 147, I thought to myself, I needed this. Life was wearing on me. I really need a mental break from the dog and job pressure I was under. Golf gave me that escape—a chance to focus intently on one thing and one thing only.

I reached into my top locker and pulled out a wire hanger. With care, I hung my khaki dress slacks on the bottom cardboard bar, and my crisp blue oxford shirt on the top. Having only worn the clothes to Mass, I wanted to wear them again without having to pay $8.50 for laundering at Kim's Cleaners. I hung the clothes up in the locker and sat for a moment on the bench wearing nothing but my boxers.

Plenty of other golfers were either finishing the day or just getting it started. Steam was floating over from the hissing showers. In various states of dress and undress, golfers were laughing with spirited razzing. Like the trendy Life is Good logo you find on ball caps and Jeep spare tire covers, life was good—for them. Sitting partially dressed and in silence, I felt stripped of joy in my life. And for such a jovial place in which I shared many golfing friends, I felt all alone.

"Come on Kevin. We're on the tee in five minutes," my pal Alan Lazzarrino prodded in his thick Brooklynese.

I stood up and started to dress. I pulled a nicely pressed adobe red polo shirt over my head, followed by the standard khaki Bermudas that every other golfer seemed to own. My black herringbone calfskin belt matched my black and white saddle shoe Footjoys.

After a quick check in the long mirror to make sure I had the outfit all put together, I reached into the back of my locker to grab some coins and golf tees out of a small box. In the pile I felt some crumpled bills that I must have thrown in weeks ago, if not months before. To my great surprise there was a twenty among the singles. It was as cool as finding forgotten cash in your jeans on wash day. It made me smile. I felt as if I hit the lottery.

Walking out of the locker room and into the golf shop, I stopped to chat with Head Pro George McNamara.

"Hey, Kevin, you want to join the Patriots Day 50-50 Lottery Raffle? Half the money goes to support the troops in Iraq and Afghanistan and half goes to the winner," he explained.

"How much is it?" I asked.

"It's twenty dollars."

Seeing how I had just found a twenty-dollar bill that I had long ago forgotten about, I felt compelled to give. I've always been a proud American. I fly the flag outside my house every day. It's how I honor my father who served in the Air Force, my grandfather before him in the Navy, and all those who've served and are serving now. It hurt to give newfound money away so fast, but it was a good kind of hurt. It just felt right.

A week later, and still in the midst of searching for a dog, I got a phone call from George McNamara. "Kevin, it's George over at the club. Hey you know that Patriots Day Raffle from last week? We just did the drawing and you won. It's $900. I'll keep the cash in the safe for you whenever you want to come in."

"Oh my God. That's awesome!" I told him. "Yeah, I'll be in later today."

"Honey," I called out to my wife, Jean.

"What?" she answered.

"Let's go ahead and get moving on a dog right away," I told her.

"What about the money?" she asked.

"I just got a great phone call from George McNamara at Brandywine. I entered a special raffle last week to raise money for the troops overseas and I won $900. That should just about cover it," I said.

"Oh my God, how lucky," Jean said as a tear streamed down her cheek and her voice quivered.

My nose started to sting. I tried to talk, but no words came out. My heart was stuck in my throat like a piece of pulp in a skinny straw. What I couldn't say in words, I said with a wink. And in a wink I was off to fetch the money that would pay for the new addition to our family.

The moment I opened the door to the Brandywine golf shop, I was shouting across the room to George McNamara. "George. George!" I called. "You're not going to believe this," I said as I approached the glass casing where the cash register sat on top.

Pressing my fingers on the glass like a defensive lineman in a four-point stance, I could see the glass fogging from the heat and the pressure beneath my fingertips. I looked up and saw George looking back at me, tripoding with his hands resting on the top of the grip of a tall golf club. "What is it?" he asked with a warm smile and an inquisitive voice.

"George, last week, I took the family out for a drive after Mass and came home and found our dog dead on the floor. It's been a really, really rough week for me, Jean, and the kids. We started looking for a new dog, but, you know, with my situation at work, I wasn't sure I could spend that kind of money. But this will either pay for it all, or most of it. Oh my God, I'm so happy," I said while taking a long, deep breath.

"Oh that's so nice," George said, "I'm really happy for you guys. Couldn't happen to a nicer family," he said nodding with approval.

George turned around and ducked into his office. His long, gray hair, which stuck out from under a navy blue Ping ball cap, followed him in. George returned with an envelope filled with a healthy stack of tens, twenties, and a couple of fifties. I shook his hand before leaving, promising to let him know how the pending purchase turned out.

I put the money and my hands in my pockets as I walked down the path from the golf shop to the parking lot. To my left by the pool, I saw the American flag sitting limp atop the flagpole in the middle of a mound. A slight gust of wind gave the Stars and Stripes a lift. The flag unfurled 30 feet above the ground. With the bright mid-afternoon sun parked almost directly above it, the bold colors that make up our flag popped even more. So did my pride in being an American and doing what good Americans should do—be generous emotionally, spiritually, and financially.

Our American flag symbolizes so many things. A simple look at it does different things to different people. On this day, I felt as if the flag, with its rise and fall in the sun and the breeze, spoke directly to me and how I was feeling. Even at rest, the flag sat restlessly, waiting for a lift that it could always count on to come. When it did, it lifted and danced the most dazzling of dances in the breezy air. That warmed my heart and lifted my spirit. Like our flag and all that it represents, sometimes we have to go through the doldrums and dark days of our own lives to realize the glory that awaits us.

Waiting for me patiently in the parking lot, about a half-wedge away from the flagpole, was my car. When I reached it, I reached into my pocket and pulled out my keys and keyless entry transmitter. Two clicks later I was entering the driver's side of my very practical white Toyota Corolla. I reached over my left shoulder with my right hand and pulled the end of the seatbelt down and across my chest, clicking into place in the receiver. I put the silver key with the black rubber top and prominent

Toyota T into the ignition. A quarter turn later the engine turned over and started to hum.

I turned on the radio to hear a voice in agony launching itself out of the AM receiver. The radio dial was set in its usual place, 610 AM WIP. It was Sunday afternoon and the Greater Philadelphia area was on edge with the Eagles. A caller was whining to Talk Show Host Angelo Cataldi about how annoyed he was with the play of then Eagles' quarterback Donovan McNabb. Angelo, who can often be as radioactive and verbally charged as a hydrogen atom, blew the guy up. "Get a life Jaah'-ree!" he shouted at a guy named Jerry from South Jersey.

"Man, I thought I had issues in my life and with McNabb," Angelo said exasperatedly to co-host Rhea Hughes, "but Jaah'-ree really needs to reevaluate what's important in his life."

That spoke to me too. What was most important in my life was appreciating the life that I had, for better or worse—and all the people, pets, pitfalls, and exultations that shaped me and colored the experience. Suddenly feeling empowered, I reached over and turned the radio off, letting silence speak louder than any shouted word could.

As I pulled the car out of the parking lot and around the semi-circle in front of the country club, I looked once more at the flag through my driver's side window. It was dancing again. I watched it do its thing in the rearview mirror until I reached the edge of the club property. Turning right on Shipley Road, I knew things were right in my life. I was moving forward with purpose and peace.

"Honey, I'm home," I announced walking in the front door. Instinctively I bent down to reach for the dog that had always come to greet me, but wasn't there anymore. The habit hadn't yet been broken. The same was true when entering my bedroom in the dark. I stepped over an invisible dog.

My reach for air at the front door that day made me smile, because with $900 in my pocket, it wouldn't be long before a new dog would be awaiting my arrival. A couple of seconds later, my arms were full for real. Samantha and Amanda were enclosed in my embrace, as Jean stood proudly behind awaiting her kiss on the cheek.

"Girls, let's go upstairs and have another look at the dogs," I said, as I pushed my pile of people toward the steps.

The staircase to the second floor of our four-bedroom Cape Cod was directly behind the front door. An old pseudo-Persian stair runner covered the wooden steps that climbed to the two bedrooms on either side of a pink-tiled Jack and Jill bathroom that was more Jill than Jack. The wall on the left side of the stairs featured framed family pictures, including a photo of me carrying puppy Tiffany on my shoulders like a shepherd does sheep.

To the left was the girls' room. To the right was the second bedroom, which was more an office than sleeping quarters. Samantha plunked herself down on the wheeled office chair that sported wicked good crayon scribble scrabble across the dimpled plastic back. Sammy gave the chair a scoot under the stained wooden desk. She slid the keyboard tray out and woke the computer monitor up by scooting the mouse across its pad. The monitor sparked to life, lighting up the room with the glow from the flat screen.

Jean and Amanda sat behind on the edge of a navy blue futon, within arm's reach of Sammy who was surfing the Web. I placed myself to Sam's right, in the same spot where a couple of days earlier I watched her looking at puppies online. The difference, this time, was the glow in my heart that matched the glow in her eyes. I knew I could pay for a new puppy. Samantha was thrilled. So was Amanda. Jean was anxious. I was relieved.

SAMANTHA

When I look for things on the computer, sometimes I go to Bing, but usually I use Google. So I went to Google and typed in "breeders for Golden Retrievers and German Shepherds." Then I started clicking on things, and all these puppies started popping up!

KEVIN

In the course of surfing around, Jean asked an interesting question. "Do Golden Retrievers shed as much as German Shepherds? I'd just like a little less vacuuming to do, because Tiffany shed so much."

"Well, I can answer that," I told her. "Goldens shed even more than Shepherds. When we had our Golden Retriever Susie, not only did hair fall off when she brushed up against something, it would just lift off her coat and float away. Goldens shed way more. Plus, the hair is more noticeable because it's red or blonde. Shepherds shed less, and their hair almost blends in with the carpets and everything else."

That's all Jean needed to hear. And the fact was, we all knew we could be happy with another German Shepherd. We were hoping to find something good in the tri-state area of Delaware, Pennsylvania, and New Jersey. Samantha's search provided fast results. We found a breeder in Nottingham, Pennsylvania, a little more than an hour's drive from our home in Northern Delaware.

Shopping for dogs online is an interesting affair. There's something voyeuristic about it. You enjoy the chance to have an intense, personal look at a living soul—from the privacy of your home. But like Internet dating, someone who looks good online is not always so attractive in person. That knowledge colors every single mouse click you make and the vision you have in your head of what one of those dogs will really be like at home.

The computer allows the extended family to join in the search and voting process. We sent out webpage links to relatives and friends for their opinions about dogs under consideration. Looking back, I don't know if that was such a good thing. If you like dozens of people second guessing you, put the word out on email, Facebook, or Twitter. You will have no shortage of people willing to take a bite.

We haven't even gotten to the issue of breeder reputability. This is where the online shopping gets tricky. A good website can make a puppy mill look like paradise. It works in reverse too. The established, trusted, and honorable breeder might come across as lesser because its website is not up to snuff. What's more, anyone can post a comment about a breeder and its dogs online.

That's good if the poster is honest, accurate, and without a vested interest in the very competitive breeding industry. Therein lies the problem. It's hard to tell who and what are credible.

In the end, we did our homework on that, but that's a story for another time. This was a family journey to find a furry, happy addition to our home. To that end, the end game was to go where we thought the best dogs were. For us, that was Amish Country in Southeastern Pennsylvania, about an hour west of Philadelphia.

Online, there were two puppy litters to choose from with the breeder we selected. As any dog owner can tell you, there's hardly such a thing as an ugly pup, so either set of Shepherds looked good to me. The litter of Gesi and Thor seemed to pique more puppy interest from Jean and the kids than the other one. Gesi was a dark, sable-colored female with bloodlines going back to the Czech Republic. Thor was a red and tan male with a godly appearance, which made perfect sense, considering he was named after the god of thunder in Norse mythology.

"Why do you like that litter more than the other one?" I asked Jean.

"Because they have more pattern on their faces and backs than the black and tan ones," Jean answered.

"Are you girls okay with Gesi and Thor's litter?" I asked the girls.

Oh, they were okay with it all right. They just wanted a dog fast, and quite frankly I did too. So I picked up the phone and made an appointment to visit the breeder. She said we could come later in the day. It was the perfect ditch from a list of honey dos.

Later in the afternoon, we loaded up our Corolla and entered the address of the breeder into our Garmin GPS. The mood was very cheerful and the girls in the back were chatty. In due diligence, while driving southwest on Route 1, I also gave further thought to Sam's suggestion to consider a boy dog. There were a couple of males and females in the litter awaiting us. Bringing another girl into the house, in essence, would make it a four-to-one ratio. In my imperfect math, I thought a male dog might even up the sides. So I called my dad on the cell phone for his advice.

"Well I just prefer the females," he said, "they're kinder, gentler, and less aggressive. That's just my choice in a type of animal."

Dad's advice confirmed what I subconsciously thought I knew already, but had pushed further back in my mind. I've been around dogs all my life, and I've loved just about all of them. I, too, always found females dogs to be more manageable. So it was time to bring another girl into our home.

"Anybody have any names for our new dog?" I asked the girls in the back.

Samantha: *"The names I thought of were Claire and Rose. But then my dad got the idea of naming her Beverly. He always names the dogs we get."*

Kevin: *"Hold on. Not always. You may get to name the next dog. But, yes, I did want to name this one Beverly. I think I'm good with dog names. I just liked the name Beverly. It gives you a lot: a nice long three-syllable name, Bev-er-ly. Or a few nicknames: Bev, Bevvers, Beverlicious, Bevster. Plus, you liked Beverly. So did Amanda and Mom."*

We were so focused on our discussion of dog names, we almost missed our exit off Route 1. The only thing that saved us was the soothing female voice on the GPS device, "In 500 feet, exit right."

When you're on a major highway in the middle of farmland, it doesn't have quite the same country feel until you get off the fast track. We followed the voice when it told us to turn right on West Christine Road. The sun reflected off the semi-smooth weathered pavement that was more whitish gray than its original black. Tall fescue grass grew on the side of the road and swayed comfortably in the gentle breeze. When a vehicle drove by, the fescue moved a little more.

Other grasses emerged where they weren't supposed to. Where there were cracks in the road, crab grass stuck out. The matted-down blades marbled the road and gave it texture. When you drove over it, the slightest change in tire elevation not only changed the feel of the drive, but also the sound. Click, clack, clacketty clack, tick, tick. It was an unpredictable rhythm that was never dull.

Because of the all the twists and turns, I really needed to put a premium on keeping my eye on the road. That wasn't easy because there really was so much to see. The attractive rolling hills of rural Pennsylvania were dotted with compressed mounds of hay that were as big as my car and resembled miniature barns. There were barns as big as football fields and others as small as a backyard shed. And everywhere you looked, there were silos. Some were Penn State blue with flat white tops. The others were tin can gray with round metal sectional tops. Rust along the ridges of each top section gave a natural color to where there was none.

If you ever wanted to paint an idyllic portrait of Amish Country, just about any view on West Christine Road would do. It's God's country in look and odor.

"Whoa, what's that smell?" Amanda asked while crinkling her cute little nose and making a sour face.

"That's good country air," I told her.

"Why does good country air smell so bad?"

"Because there's manure in the fields," I explained.

"What's manure?" Amanda went on.

"It's cow chips, or animal waste."

"What are cow chips and animal waste?"

"It's cow poop."

"Why don't they clean it up?"

"They spread it on the fields to fertilize the soil. It makes the crops grow better. You know Miracle Grow, the magic stuff that Mommy puts in the flower pots at home?"

"Yes."

"It's kind of like that, but it's free."

While explaining farming 101 to the kids, I felt a slight bump under the car. "What was that?" I asked.

Samantha looked out the back window. "Uh, Dad, I think you just drove over a cow chip," she said followed by a giggle attack.

Mounds on the roads of Chester and Lancaster counties tell you all you need to know about who was traveling around here and how they're doing it. The Amish do not use motorized transportation or electricity. They dress simply, go to their own country schools, and live a humble, religious life. They work the land the old-fashioned way, with oxen-drawn plows in the fields.

As we reached the crest of the road, our scanning eyes came directly into focus with a horse and buggy moving slowly. An orange triangle reflector trimmed in red was on the back of the black carriage signaling that it was a "slow moving" vehicle.

At the front was a black malt-colored horse trotting along at a clop, clop, clop pace. Holding the leather reins and steering the horse was a man in his thirties with a banded straw hat and a modest dark blue shirt with suspenders. He had a beard, but no mustache. Like me, he had a wife and two small children. He drove with a purpose. I don't know where he was going, but he was determined to get there.

Sitting to the Amish man's right in the buggy was his wife. Her hair was pulled back in a tight bun covered by a simple veiled bonnet. Her dress was a lighter shade of blue than her husband's shirt. She was pretty in a simple way, like Kelly McGillis in the film *Witness*.

The couple's two girls were dressed nearly identical to their mom and looked more like her than him. During the ride, the girls seemed more interested in looking around than their parents, who just looked straight ahead.

I drove by slowly, not wanting to spook the horse and to be respectful of their private Amish lifestyle. I glanced over and saw one of the Amish children looking at us out of the back side window of the buggy. In the rearview mirror, I saw Amanda turn to find the wide eyes of the little Amish girl who was about her age. Amanda smiled and the girl in the buggy smiled back.

The peaceful picture of the Amish family we passed on the road was in direct contrast to a visual I still have ingrained in my head from the last time I visited Pennsylvania Dutch Country. Almost two years to the day, I was smack in the middle of one of the most tragic events our country and this countryside had ever seen. It was October 2, 2006, when a troubled milk truck driver, thirty-two-year-old Charles Roberts, IV, burst into an Amish school house. He was armed with a shotgun and other weapons. He ordered the boys out and tied up ten young school girls.

Roberts was mad at God, and the sight of other young girls further twisted his tortured soul. Years earlier, his daughter died just twenty minutes after birth. Those who knew him say Roberts never got over it. Survivors of the shooting say he told the girls they were going to have to pay for what happened to his daughter. With a cold heart he then went about the execution process. Five of the girls died, the others survived, despite horrific wounds from shotgun blasts at pointblank range. Satisfied with his efforts, Roberts then turned the gun on himself and took his own life.

When I came to cover the news story for my network the day after the shootings, the Pennsylvania State Police kept the hundred or so media members about a quarter mile away from the West Nickel Mines schoolhouse on White Oak Road. The intersection of Mine Road and White Oak Road really was a crossroads of life. Once the place of the quiet simple life, Nickel Mines in Lancaster County found itself in the middle of a world it never wanted.

There were at least twenty satellite news trucks lining the road. Reporters had cell phones stuck to their ears. TV news photographers were lifting heavy cameras onto tripods and shooting in the direction of the clearing in the corn where the schoolhouse shooting happened. Every fifteen minutes or so, the familiar sound of horse hooves clopping on the road would snap everybody to attention. Along would come a horse and buggy, always driven by a bearded man who looked as if he was lost despite knowing the country roads by heart.

The scene repeated itself several times during the day, but there was one buggy passing that stood out and crushed me. I was standing-by, locked in position just a couple of seconds away from doing a live report on TV. I was thinking about what to say and how to say it. I heard the now familiar horse steps getting closer.

As I turned my head to the right, I saw a young Amish boy sitting next to his father. The boy turned his head in my direction. Our eyes locked. He couldn't have been more than seven or eight years old. He looked so sad and stunned. Maybe he was one of the boys the gunman ordered out of the schoolhouse before attacking the girls. I'll never know. But I do know this—nobody should have to feel the kind of pain that provoked that boy's expression.

In a quick change of editorial content, I talked about the boy on the air. I just thought it was a different way to express the magnitude of the tragedy. I don't know if it worked, but I still think about it. I just can't get the vision of that boy in the buggy out of my head. I see him in my mind's eye, and I get the chills just thinking about it.

"Daddy, why are those people riding in that black wagon behind the horse?" Amanda wanted to know.

"Because that's how Amish people travel. They don't have cars like we do," I told her.

"But isn't that really slow? Wouldn't it take a long time to get to school or somewhere else?" she asked.

"Yes, the horse and buggy don't move very fast. But usually they don't go far from home. They have their own special Amish school, which is usually within walking distance."

The questions about the Amish lifestyle followed us up the steep hill. It was a joy to answer them and even better to see happy Amish times once again. Even though we were a long buggy ride away from Nickel Mines, Amish people are exceptionally close, and the tragedy of that day touched Amish communities everywhere. But, just like the Amish elders who found it best to tear down the scarred West Nickel Mines School and build a new school called New Hope, hope had returned to Amish country. You could see it in the famously stoic Amish demeanor and feel it in your heart.

After reaching the crest of the hill and starting down the other side, we saw a different Amish family going about their day, which, considering it was Sunday, involved more rest around the house and property than work.

"Why do their clothes look so different from ours?" Sammy wanted to know.

"Because they prefer a simple look," I told her. "They make their own clothes. They don't have sewing machines like we do. In fact, they don't even have electricity inside their homes."

"Wait, you mean they don't have lights inside their house?" Amanda interrupted.

"That's right," I said.

"Well, how do they see when it's dark in their house?" Samantha followed.

"They have lanterns and candles to find their way around in the dark. But they go to bed much earlier than we do and they get up earlier. They do most of their work and play when it's light out."

"So they don't have TV?" Amanda asked in mock horror.

"No, they don't have TV."

"Oh my gosh! I don't know if I could live without TV," Amanda gushed.

"Amanda, honey, you'd be fine without TV," Jean said joining the conversation.

"Yeah, in fact less TV might be better for you," I suggested.

That sent Amanda into a little tizzy, which didn't last long because it was time to make a right turn, and then a fast left into the breeder's driveway.

SAMANTHA

I remember pulling into the breeder's driveway and seeing the sign that said E-Z Brook Kennels. It was rocky and crunchy, not like our smooth driveway back in Delaware. The land looked like nice countryside. There was a big fence, a wire fence. There were lots of big dogs to help the puppies. There was barking when we came walking up to the breeder's house. It was loud. There was a little tub that was blue and it belonged to the puppies. There was a small smell of dogs, but it was okay.

KEVIN

I remember the barking of the dogs as something close to a roar. I don't know how quiet it was prior to our arrival, but the place really came alive when we got out of the car. When Susie the breeder greeted us, I said, "So I take it security is never a problem around here is it?"

"Oh no, we're well taken care of," Susie said with a laugh.

A medium-sized female German Shepherd came over to the fence for a closer look. Her name was Dolly. She was sweet and was fishing for attention. There were other dogs that would've come over, but the fencing pattern wouldn't allow it. They barked instead. Susie led us to an enclosed part of the kennel where the litter of Gesi and Thor was resting inside an igloo. Susie woke them up and out they wobbled, still feeling the funk from being awakened.

SAMANTHA

They were so cute. I wanted to have all of them. I thought that someday when I grow up and get married, I would have eight children, and each child would have their own dog. We'd all live in a mansion and the puppies would have babies. That way we'd have even more puppies with lots of land to play on. I would not give away the puppies that were born.

All of the dogs at the breeder's house wanted to play with me outside of their igloo. The one part that was bad was that they nipped my pants and my legs. It really hurt, but not so bad to make me cry.

KEVIN

Amanda got nipped too. We all did, as the puppies swarmed like bees in a hive. The half dozen pups jumped, low-bridged, bulldozed and bit littermates all while vying for our attention. It was crazy, but fun and dirty. Amanda had a glob of something on the cuff of her purple corduroys. It was hard for Jean to wipe it off because of the lines in the pants. My recently buffed black loafers were covered with muddy paw prints. We all had slobber on our hands and clothes, but this is what we came for.

After about ten minutes or so, Jean and I had our eye on two of the girl puppies. The breeder put different colored collars on them so they'd be easier to mark and track in the flurry around us. It was between the purple collar and the pink one. We went with purple. Susie asked us to come with her inside the house so we could see our selected dog's parents.

As we walked away from the puppy area and toward the house, the remaining dogs in the outside kennels started to sing. Over the roar, Susie leaned in and shouted "Do any of you have illegal or prescription drugs on you?"

"No," I answered, "why do you ask?"

"Because we have a narcotics detection dog on the premises, and he will hit on it if he smells something," she said.

"What does he do when he finds drugs? Does he sit down?"

"No, he bites," Susie said cautiously while gesturing to a large dog behind her by the back door.

I looked over Susie's shoulder and saw Argus looking right back at me. I'm not sure he was looking at me as much as he was looking through me. It was a visual scolding. Argus was large and almost completely black on top. He had a gentle brush of tan between his eyes and on his cheeks, but there was nothing else that looked gentle about him. If looks could kill, Argus was an assassin.

Susie brought us into her basement, which tripled as an indoor kennel, showroom, and office. Behind portable fencing was a couch covered with a white sheet. It was the resting place for three dogs who immediately perked up when we the people wandered in from the outside. Nary an eye wandered from us. There was Thor, Magnum, and Krista. They were not a pride, but they had the pride of lions and heads to match. It was clear this was not the place to wander without an escort from Susie, their de facto Alpha dog.

I liked the feeling of protection German Shepherds gave and thought we could duplicate it at our house. All we needed was one of the big boys' little girls.

To our right was a small female Shepherd inside a kennel with the door closed. Her name was Gesi. Gesi was a sable-colored girl who looked weary and exhausted. When we learned she had just finished nursing much of her litter, the look about her made sense. She wasn't sad, she was dog-tired.

So that we could better see where our future dog descended from, Susie called Thor over from the couch. He obediently came right away, stood up on his hind legs, and dropped his heavy front paws onto Susie's shoulders. He was as tall as she was, but clearly submissive to her. He looked into her eyes and flicked his tongue at her nose in a kiss.

I didn't want that kind of facial, but I wanted to pet him. Thor came right over with an attractive confidence, lifted his eyes toward mine, and buried his nose in the palm of my hand. As I petted him, he leaned to the side toward the children, giving off a vibe that called them over. The kids loved him. I have to hand it to Thor—he was as cool as his name.

Totally convinced that we picked the right puppy for us based on her looks, disposition, and her desirable parents, we told the breeder we were ready to buy the dog we'd call Beverly. We paid in cash. Jean asked for a receipt.

Susie said, "Wait right here. I'll have to run upstairs and get one."

When Susie went upstairs, we were left all alone. Not that we would have done anything wrong, but while Susie was gone, the dogs seemingly switched on an internal alert. We were put on notice.

To my right, I saw Argus staring a hole through me. He never moved and I'm not sure he even blinked. I probably didn't either. It was as intimidating as a girl's tough father answering the door on her first date. But Argus was true to his training. He would do nothing unless you gave him a reason.

Amanda Walsh is eight. She's Samantha's sister, daughter of Kevin and Jean and granddaughter of Grandpops Bob. She is currently helping raise Beverly, also pictured here as a pup.

Soon Susie returned with a receipt. She went outside, scooped up our new dog, and placed her in Samantha's arms. Of course Amanda wanted to help carry Beverly home at the same time. So, in something of a team hug-and-carry, the two girls slid sideways out the back door with Beverly sandwiched between them pecking away at their hands. It was painfully darling.

We got to the car and the three girls climbed into the backseat. Beverly was in between them running in a tight circle, but occasionally expanding the orbit to include their laps. There was a constant giggle interrupted by an occasional "ouch!" from the girls and a squeak from the dog.

While retracing our journey through the countryside and back to the highway, we passed the same property where earlier we saw an Amish family gathered around the house and enjoying a relaxing Sunday. The parents were sitting on a bench having something cold to drink. A boy was sitting on the edge of the wooden porch, playing fetch with his dog. He would throw a stick and the black-and-white Retriever mix would happily return it.

In an instant, my mind flashed back to two years ago, when I saw a different Amish boy who was distraught and riding in the buggy with his dad near the West Nickel Mines schoolhouse. I thought if ever there was a child who could use a dog to lift his spirits, that boy in the buggy was the one.

"Look girls. See the Amish family over there?" I asked, making sure not to point. "They have a dog too. See how much joy that dog brings the boy on the porch?"

"Did they get their dog from Susie?" Amanda asked.

"No, I don't think so. Susie just has German Shepherds and Corgis," I answered.

"Well, at least they have a dog to play with," Sammy said, "and now we have one again too."

Beverly, 2008

It was a lovely thing to say. It validated the purchase and made all the work, travel, and research in finding our new dog worthwhile. Seeing the joy that their dog brought to the Amish family reminded me of how happy my past dogs made me feel, and how excited I was to have Beverly a part of our future.

I reached up to adjust the rearview mirror's tilt. I caught Beverly looking right into my eyes. She gave her tail a wag and her head a tilt. I just melted. I grabbed Jean's hand, looked into her eyes, motioning with my head to look in the mirror too. Her jaw dropped, and she gave my hand a squeeze. With her other hand she tapped gently on her heart. She couldn't speak, but she didn't have to. She really had said it all.

Beverly has grown into a lovely dog. She is the consummate companion and protector of our house and family. As much as we wanted another Tiffany—in terms of breed and temperament—Beverly is a whole different animal in more ways than one. Part of that comes from the breeding lines. The rest is the result of how we raise her.

As best we can tell, Tiffany, our first German Shepherd, was a backyard breed. There's no lengthy list of who her parents and grandparents were, what they did and where they came from. Tiffany loved to play, and if given a job she would do it. But more than anything, she was a hang-out dog.

Tiffany spent a lot of time alone. When we got her, both Jean and I were working. There was a doggy door that led to our fenced backyard, so Tiffany could come and go as she pleased. When we were home, Tiffany would sit with us for hours and rarely demanded anything. She was independent and lacked the legendary German Shepherd drive.

Beverly definitely has the drive, and then some. She's a sweetie with an edge. I have no doubt the edge comes from her parents' working lines that extend back to Europe generations before. When protective, Beverly is a brute. I pity the fool who would ever be foolish enough to break into our house. Bev would eviscerate him. She can rumble.

But Beverly is also very needy. She craves a lot of affection. If you don't offer it, she'll more or less impose herself upon you. She's a face licker. It can be very intimidating, if you don't know her. I've seen many a look of horror from others when Beverly's toothy mouth opens during a greeting. The worst a friendly person will ever get is a wet kiss, but even then, it's a bit much. We're trying to break her of the habit, but we're not having much luck.

Tiffany loved to be petted by everyone, but she didn't like it when children became face invaders. Beverly has no personal space issues at all. She's had someone in her face her whole life and doesn't see it as an invasion. My girls will press their noses against hers and pick the gook out of the corners of her eyes. To Beverly, that's as natural as a pat on the top of her head and a stroke down her back. She doesn't back off one bit. She is her own personal "Please Touch Museum."

When Bev needs something, she'll make it clear. If she needs to go out, she'll crowd you and cry till you heed the call. When hungry, she'll pick up her bowl and drop it at your feet. If she wants to play, she'll find a ball and badger you until you give in. She's easy to read because she's so expressive. With Beverly, we've given our children their first crack at real life responsibility.

SAMANTHA

Ever since we moved to Massachusetts when I was eight years old, I've been taking care of Beverly. I take her for walks and feed her. I take her up to the Italo American Club near my school. She likes to sniff around and go to the bathroom in the tall grass. I have to bring bags to pick up after her. Sometimes it's really messy and I can't pick all the poop up. I usually tell my parents and they help me. Daddy says it's important to pick up after your dog. People want to keep their property clean. If you don't pick up after your dog, people could step in it. It makes their shoes dirty.

KEVIN

Beyond our family's personal responsibilities for the dog, there are community obligations too. As much as my father (Grandpops Bob) cringes when I talk and write about poop, the fact of the matter is there are lessons to be learned from it. Is there any greater violation than letting your dog relieve itself on someone else's grass, or public property, without having the decency to clean it up? I don't think so.

But wait, there's more. The cleanup process is rarely clean, and there are lessons to pick up from the pickup. Fecal matter is packed with germs and bacteria. Remember how our parents and teachers hounded us to always wash our hands after we went to the bathroom? Really, how many of us listened? I know I didn't. Add dogs to the mix and you have another opportunity to emphasize the need for good hygiene and cleaning habits.

"Make sure you wash your hands really good when you're done picking up after the dog," my dad insisted, when I was a boy.

Who knew it would take a dog for me to reach the tipping point in my own bathroom endeavors? Thanks, Dad!

An editorial meeting

Bob "Grandpops": *"I don't know why you have to talk about things like that."*

Kevin: *"Dad, c'mon! Don't be such a stiff. So we don't agree on what's good descriptive language. That's probably our generation gap once again. But we're clear with the life lessons and responsibility that dogs teach us, right? It's not unlike how uncomfortable you felt when Samantha described finding Tiffany dead on the floor and how much it hurt her heart. We may never agree on the subject matter and word choice, but we can most certainly accept that dogs provoke and touch us in so many different ways."*

Samantha: *"Daddy, are you and Grandpops having an argument?"*

Kevin: *"No, no, no, honey. We're just having a creative discussion. Someday, you and I will have them too."*

Taking the dog for a walk isn't just a moment shared between you and the pet. It's a public event. Every time our children take Beverly outside, she must be on a leash. That's our rule. We know that not everyone "gets" and loves dogs like we do. We need to be respectful of that, and we are.

Beverly plants one on a pal before going to the dog park, Wellesley, Mass., 2010

Dogs give us leadership and obedience opportunities to experiment with. I tell Samantha to take charge with Beverly and to be firm with commands. It took some time for it all to come together, but now Sammy's got it and so does Bev. It's a beautiful thing to look out the window and see Samantha and Beverly walking down the sidewalk enjoying each other's company. Sammy leads from a position of strength and doesn't abuse her authority. Beverly respects that. It's an honorable dynamic.

Then there's the dog park. We don't have an "official" fenced-in park in our neighborhood, but the Sprague ballfields do the job just fine. On most mornings between seven and nine you will often see a pack of dogs at play. It's social hour for creatures on four legs and two.

Don is here with Arby, the Jack Russell Terrier with a Boston Bruins dog collar. Frances brought Meggie, a small black Lab mix who'd rather play mother hen than go for a run. Jim is smoking a cigar while keeping an eye on Latilda, a dark tan mystery mix breed. Lattie, as most of us call Latilda, mixes well with the other dogs. She's not overly energetic and doesn't have to be. She's cool and she knows it, kind of like Jim.

Because I work nights, getting up early to visit the dog park isn't easy. Sometimes I take the kids. They love to visit with other dogs. It's also a good lesson for Sammy and Amanda to witness the importance of group play and social interaction (among humans and animals). That interaction starts before we actually join the group.

As we approach the park, Beverly lowers her body and peels her tall ears back. Her approach is slow, deliberate, and cautious. Some dogs are thrilled to see her, wagging their tails in delight. Other dogs are more reticent. The dog owners ape their pets' feelings. Whatever the reception, we try to make the best of it and make sure Beverly is a good guest.

Sometimes the dogs get into it. On a chilly day in November 2010, Beverly found herself on the receiving end. She was running with two other dogs of about equal size. With little warning, the play turned into a spirited two-on-one that included zigzagging between the forest and the tennis courts. The other dogs had Bev sandwiched in between, and they were nipping at her head and hindquarters. Beverly ran fast to separate herself, but the boxing-in left her no place to go. The gnashing of teeth and barking intensified.

Beverly's head was soon covered with globs of spit. Her usual sleek and smooth fur was disheveled, and you could see lines in her coat where claws and sharp teeth had left their mark. The tone of Beverly's barking changed quickly. It was more a cry for mercy.

Beverly usually doesn't need much help because typically she's the biggest dog at the park. There have been a few occasions when she's taken advantage of that, roughing up other dogs by herself, or with the help of a co-conspirator. Seeing her in distress was certainly not a welcome thing, but I thought it might be a good lesson for her to get a taste of her own bullying. This, however, quickly turned from a minor dustup to full blown butt-kicking. Repeated efforts to break the dogs up with shouting failed.

Beverly ran for the baseball field where the beating continued on the infield dirt between second and third base. The other dogs worked in tandem. One blocked in front while the other attacked from behind—launching itself in a flying tackle onto Beverly's hips, causing her back legs to buckle and give out. Bev fell down, got up, yelped out in pain, and endured at least two more repeats of canine assault.

In a matter of seconds, the moving fight had made its way out deeper into left field. The others dogs were crashing into a tiring Beverly, T-boning her from the sides, forcing her to roll over. Dizzy from the spinning, Beverly had little defense for the dog on the other side who now had a free shot at Bev as she lay on her back. It was getting really scary, as I raced across the first base line, shouting the whole way.

Usually, Beverly runs to me on command. On this day I don't even think she heard my voice. She was cowering before the other dogs who were drunk on adrenaline and unwilling to relent. Somehow, in the course of the stomping, slobbering, and semi-mauling, Beverly flipped over, landed on all fours, and made a break for it in the direction of the maintenance shed over by the artificial turf football field. The other dogs were trailing her, but not by much.

By the time I had reached the outfield, I had lost sight of the dogs. On the line I'd last seen them traveling, they were only about 150 yards away from the very busy Route 9, and moving quickly in that direction.

"Beverly! Beverly!" I called over and over again in full sprint. No sign of the dogs.

After passing the maintenance shed and making a right turn around the corner, which opens into the Sprague School parking lot, I saw one of the aggressive dogs heading back toward me. With his owner following right behind me, the dog just went right on by. I kept going. Still, no sign of Beverly.

After crossing the parking lot I followed the footpath through the brush on the forest's edge, which leads to the old neighborhood where we rented a home by the intersection of Stearns and Francis Roads. We were 50 yards away now from Route 9 and I could hear the loud traffic whizzing by.

"Beverly!" I called while bounding through the trees and up Stearns Road, which parallels Route 9.

I thought Beverly might have run to the old neighborhood thinking it would be a safe haven. Turned out it was. By the time I was halfway up Stearns Road, I heard, "She's over here."

I looked to my right and there was Beverly standing on the side stoop of the home of family friends. My pal Vincent said, "Beverly came running up the driveway, but the other dog stopped at the street. He wouldn't come up."

Beverly and Chance, backyard play date, 2011

Maybe he knew better. Beverly was looking in the glass window of Vincent's door at the dog on the other side. Inside was Chance, her boyfriend, a black Lab mix whom she's shared many a play date, walks, and kisses. Beverly looked tired but hardly as traumatized as she was just a few moments before. I rounded her up, thanked Vincent, and started walking home across the Sprague fields.

On the far side of field, I bumped into another of the dog owners who witnessed what transpired. "Is your dog okay? I just feel so bad for you guys," she said.

"She's fine," I told her, "I guess it was just one of those things where the other dogs just got so intoxicated in the attack, they lusted for more. Maybe I should have intervened sooner, before it escalated to the level it did."

We both felt bad, but not so bad that we didn't bring our dogs back to the park to play again. Sometimes life gets ugly in an instant. That's the teachable moment. We saw it that day. I think all of us dog owners will be more vigilant to make sure future roughhousing doesn't grow into something ugly and unmanageable. It's all part of the deal.

I tell my daughters there are lessons to be learned from the dog park mosh pit. Sometimes friends get on each other's nerves and take it out on each other. Or a new person enters the mix and disrupts the chemistry. Usually, I think, it's best for the kids to work through the issues themselves. But if it's more than they can handle, it's time for the parents to get involved. What we see at the dog park isn't much different than what they see in their classrooms and on the playground. It's just a different cast of characters.

At home, there's no shortage of activity to capture Beverly's attention. In front of our house, there's always someone walking to school or going in the other direction toward Roche Brothers grocery store and the Linden Street Shops. Out back, there's a bevy of wildlife: squirrels, chipmunks, moles, birds, and the occasional fox. The storm door window is a window to the world. But, really, Bev's world is much more about where we (her family) are than anything else.

.   .   .

Amanda comforts Beverly, 2010

Samantha: *"Those dogs who beat up Beverly were bullies. I don't like bullies."*

Kevin: *"Nobody does, Sammy."*

Samantha: *"Were Grandpops and Uncle Dicky bullies for beating up the boy who made fun of Uncle Dicky's handicap?"*

Kevin: *"Uh, you want to handle this one, Dad?"*

Bob "Grandpops": *"No. The boy was a bully for picking on a kid with polio. It was a different time back then. We took care of it, and never had a problem with that bully again."*

Kevin with Samantha and Amanda and Beverly, 2009

If I am outside doing yard work, Beverly insists on being there with me. If the children are playing out back, Beverly will have a fit if she can't be by their side. Her whining is overwhelming. It sounds like a dog being abused. I've found it really is best to just give in to her. All she wants is to be with her family, which she loves so much.

Beverly is a shadow who follows you around. Going to the bathroom? She'll be there—sometimes a little too close. Taking a shower? She'll be the mat. Need a pillow? I don't use her for that, but the kids do. She is everywhere you look because she doesn't want to miss anything that involves us. She is omnipresent, available for anything, and that is why we love her.

TWELVE

To Future Dogs
and Future Generations

BOB, SAMANTHA AND KEVIN

Samantha: *"I would love to have lots of dogs when I grow up. It is really fun to love them and pet them. I will live in a mansion so there's room for everybody—all my dogs, eight kids, and my husband."*

Kevin: *"Whoa, wait a minute. Eight kids and a mansion? How are you going to afford all that, Sammy?"*

Samantha: *"Maybe we can have a lot of lemonade stands and raise the money."*

Kevin: *"Do you think people will come to your lemonade stands because the lemonade tastes so good, or because you're so cute?"*

Samantha: *"Maybe both. If I live in a big mansion I'll probably need some German Shepherds because robbers love to rob really big houses. German Shepherds are good dogs, very strong, alert, and protective. I'd like a few German Shepherds guarding the house. I'll feel safer that way.*

"I'd like to start with a few puppies. When they're older and ready to have their own puppies, I'll be happy. I'd also like to

stay away from the animals when they have their babies. I like to give them peace, quiet, and privacy. A friend of mine told me that if you watch dogs having their puppies, they will get angry and be aggressive with you. It is not very pleasant to watch, but I'd love to take care of them.

"When I grow up, I also want to be a veterinarian and take care of the animals. I like that job because animals are so cute. I don't want them to be sick or injured, so that is why I will grab the job. I know that it is a big job, but I would love to do it."

Kevin: *"Sammy is a dreamer and I like that about her. Dreamers always have hope. Without hope you have nothing. We'll see if she gets that big ole mansion, handsome man, bevy of kids, and a pack of dogs. At the very least I have no doubt she'll have at least one dog of her own, when it's time to be on her own. This gives my heart a lift. And I'm not alone. Hey, Dad. How does it make you feel to know that the gift of dogs that your dad gave you, and you gave to us, will live to see another generation?"*

Bob "Grandpops": *"It makes me feel good."*

Kevin: *"That's it?"*

Bob "Grandpops": *"What do you want me to say?"*

Kevin: *"Actually that was beautiful. You said a lot in a little."*

Samantha Walsh, Agunquit Beach, Maine, 2011

Looking back there are so many what ifs in our lives and journey. What if I had not won the Patriots Day Raffle? What if I had not purchased a dog with the winnings? What if I had not lost my job and then found another? Ultimately all roads lead back to Atwood Street, where Beverly got a whiff of something good. Quite simply, we followed the dog home.

. . .

The Tail End

Kevin, Amanda, Samantha and Beverly,
Wellesley, Mass., 2010

KEVIN

I always thought the discovery of my father's childhood home with the help of my German Shepherd Beverly was one of those really cool things that was just meant to be—almost like Susie the Golden Retriever finding the other Kevin Walsh at college. But when a coworker of mine wondered if Beverly's doing might be rooted in science, I dug deeper. His curiosity piqued my interest, and I figured others would want to know too.

So I checked with prominent veterinary researchers. From what we can tell, there is no solid evidence that Beverly has found seventy-year-old family DNA. She's getting a whiff of something good on Atwood Street—it's just not Dad's skin flakes dating back to 1941. She might be picking up on my feelings and a vibe that I give off. I don't know, and it hardly matters. Ultimately, Beverly paved the road that gave us a good look at Dad's old house, and that made all the difference.

We finished our journey in the writing of this book in the same place where it started. If that makes it seem as if we were really organized, let me tell you something— we weren't even close! We were all over the place. At times, I wasn't sure it would all come together. But that's the beauty of a worthwhile journey. Overcoming rough spots and detours made it much more meaningful. Dad, Samantha, and I finished as changed people, better people.

We learned a lot about life on our two legs from our friends who walk on four. We added information to the storylines, subtracted from a few, and when other family members unearthed new nuggets for us, we dropped them in. There was no shortage of helpers when folks found out what we were up to.

The book itself started out with my dad dabbling in writing on his own. He called me up on the phone one night and shared the news that he was writing a book.

"Really? About what?" I asked.

"Dogs. I'm writing about my dogs, all the dogs I've had," he said.

"That's cool," I told him, "what are you going to do with it when you're done?"

"I'll just write the book, and I'll have you publish it for me."

It was as simple as that. What my dad didn't realize was getting published is hardly simple, as I discovered when I wrote *The Marrow in Me* in 2009. Dad wasn't worried though; publishing was my problem.

I suggested Dad add something beyond the dogs themselves, and more than one voice. That's when *Follow the Dog Home* became a family project. The concept of dogs as "institutions," connectors of generations, and teachers of life's profound lessons were added. Samantha and I joined the writing process.

I knew we had cool stories, but I never imagined my dogs would lead me to places that I never knew existed, and into unbelievably guarded places where intensely personal feelings held by my dad, my mother, my brothers, my wife, and my children secretly lived. I thought I knew, but it turns out I really didn't know much at all.

We didn't just *Follow the Dog Home*, as the book title suggests; our dogs helped us discover the family that we are, not the one we imagined ourselves to be.

I told my dad to be vulnerable, to reveal a personal side in his writing that many of us didn't know existed. He didn't give it up easily. I'll never forget pulling him aside during Thanksgiving dinner in 2010. We were at my stepbrother Joe McGrattan's house in Avon, Connecticut.

After dinner, Dad and I went to the enclosed patio to talk quietly. I wanted the conversation to uncover what he and I could write about later. We talked about some of his life's greatest losses, including family members and dogs. He couldn't wait for that talk to be over. He also wanted another crack at the chocolate cake Joe and Cambrya McGrattan had made.

In the end, it was clear to me that Dad is probably most at peace with himself, and the world, when a dog is by his side. He lets his dogs express feelings for him. As unique as he is, there are millions of people just like him in that regard.

My daughter Samantha, on the other hand, has no problem expressing herself. She's affectionate and articulate. I think part of the reason has to do with all the practice she's had interacting and role-playing with our dogs over the years.

In February 2011, Samantha and Amanda went to their first funeral. Parents with small kids know how tricky that can be. The loss of our first German Shepherd, Tiffany, a few years before, gave them a perspective to draw from. Both girls showed the appropriate level of sadness and maturity and had no trouble talking with the many adults who were there.

One of our greatest hopes in writing this book was that readers—assuming most are dog lovers—would vicariously see a part of their own lives and families through us, letting their personal experiences parallel ours, in their hearts and minds. This happens quite naturally, when people are engaged in interesting conversation and reading.

Something else, if you haven't spent time with your family in thoughtful conversation with meaningful bonding experiences, won't you try again soon? Simply talking to your parents, grandparents, children, and siblings about the family dog or dogs or other pets is a wonderful conversation starter; it can soothe wounds, uncover family history, and restore or start a family connection you've always wished for.

Let me give you a few examples: If I hadn't told my Aunt Jean (Walsh) Bryant about my gravitation toward the home on Atwood Street, it's unlikely she would have told me that my father—unbeknownst even to him—briefly lived in that same house as an infant. Details and history such as that hardly seemed to matter—until a dog walked into the picture and changed everything.

Here's another example: My dad never knew that his first dog Dee Dee was poisoned by a heartless neighbor. That was revealed in a conversation with Dad's older sister Boots decades later. A shocker!

And a final story: If I hadn't looked over Samantha's shoulder while she sat typing at the computer, I never would have known that the joy for her new dog, Beverly, was juxtaposed to the guilt of moving on after the death of her previous dog, Tiffany. I'm so proud of Sammy, and I love her for her loyalty.

Dogs lead us, love us, protect us, and help us reflect on the most profound moments of our lives. Ask folks what their dog means to them on a personal level; you just might spark a sentiment that reaches into their innermost sanctum.

There's something special about the positive printed word looking back at you. You can't escape it, especially when those words capture your soul. It's like looking at your dog, which mirrors your truest feelings in expression and thought. I hope *Follow the Dog Home* will touch your heart and soul as much as it did ours to write it. Thank you for coming on our family journey. God bless.

Acknowledgments

So many people contributed to *Follow the Dog Home*, and for that we're eternally grateful. What we started with is certainly not what we finished with—and don't we know. Things evolve in the writing, assembling, and editing processes. Family, friends, and publishing professionals provided insights that enriched our book.

We'd like to thank Marie Beth "Boots" Hall, Wayne Smolda, Joy Renjilian-Burgy of Wellesley College, and Jean Gnap for their superb reviews and suggestions. They shared their time and talents simply because we asked, and because they love us. We love them back.

We'd also like to thank our family members who uncovered pictures we'd lost track of and shared memories we had forgotten. Family historians Jean (Walsh) Bryant and "Boots" (Walsh) Hall took us back in time to make sense of pictures that were mysterious to us. They provided the necessary background and context that made our chosen stories sing. Chris and Michael Walsh generously shared stories of their dogs and dug up pictures that had long ago fallen into the abysses of cluttered basements and attics.

Daisy and Rio, Chris Walsh's current dogs

Our wives and siblings were very special to us in the writing process with patience and understanding when we needed time away from family to work on the book.

Bob would like to thank his wife, Mary, for her love and encouragement. Kevin would like to thank his wife, Jean, who not only ran the house while Kevin disappeared in the family office for hours at a time, she also regularly popped in, offered support, advice, and technical expertise time and time again when the computer crashed. Samantha would like to thank her parents and sister, Amanda, for encouraging her to be brave and loving while writing her first book.

We'd like to thank Stacey Miller of Bookpr.com for her guidance and encouragement as we started our journey.

We'd like to thank our neighbor and friend Susan Fay, the Wayland Middle School English teacher who provided a key nugget of clarity in a time and place where it was greatly needed.

We'd like to thank David Wright and Pamela Bristah for welcoming us back to where our journey with dogs started all those years ago. They were so kind to us and treated us like family.

We are so grateful to the good people and professionals at Concierge Marketing and Publishing: Lisa Pelto and her team Ellie, Erin, and Gary, and our editor Sandra Wendel. They superbly guided us through the publishing process.

Of course we collectively thank all of our dogs for the years of love and companionship they've given us. We followed the dog home, and home is always a better place when a dog is there.

Praise for
Follow the Dog Home

"If you love dogs, or if you like people who love dogs, you will love this deeply human chronicle of a family and its dogs."

Rabbi Harold Kushner,
author of *When Bad Things Happen to Good People*

"I often say there's only one greatest pet in the world and every family has that pet. What I love about this unique book is the detailed story of 17 'greatest' pets and three generations of a family that loves pets like family. Woven over almost three quarters of a century, the constant drumbeats of this book are the value that pets bring families in making us feel good and being good for us and how dogs are connection catalysts. In this increasingly high-tech world where families are often far flung, nothing helps young and old to bond quite like the love of dogs."

Dr. Marty Becker, "America's Veterinarian,"
author of 20 pet books and anchor of Vetstreet.com

"We have this wonderful spiritual and emotional connection to our dogs these days, they are treasured members of our families. Our dogs teach us something every day, something that reaches everyone in the family and endures for generations. This wonderful book by the Walshes shows that home, indeed, is where the dog is. Snuggle up on the couch with your dog by your side and have a happy read of this great family story."

David Frei, author of *Angel on a Leash*, and the voice of the Westminster Kennel Club and the National Dog Show

"After raising three Golden Retrievers, I've always said it's a dog's world, and the rest of us are just visiting. Kevin Walsh's heart-warming new book proves my point."

Jackie MacMullan, ESPN Commentator, Hall of Fame Basketball Writer, author of *When the Game Was Ours* and *Shaq: Uncut*

"Leave it to a dog to evoke the best in three generations' feelings of compassion, family, and humor. Kevin Walsh brings home poignant messages without hitting us over the head with them. This book is a treat for humans."

Mary Mitchell, author of *The Complete Idiot's Guide to Etiquette*, Nationally Syndicated Columnist, owner of Zsa Zsa the French Bulldog

"If you own a dog, you'll understand. If you don't own a dog, maybe this will bring you on board. Dogs bring us together and connect generations every bit as much as baseball or old family homesteads. Kevin, Bob, and Samantha Walsh connect all the dots in *Follow the Dog Home*. They are the dog whisperers."

Dan Shaughnessy, author of *The Curse of the Bambino*
and *Boston Globe* columnist

"Get me one of those dogs!"

Mike Felger, Boston Radio & TV Host, owner of Lab Lucky